PUBLICATIONS OF THE UNIVERSITY OF MANCHESTER

HISTORICAL SERIES
No. XXXVII

LETTERS OF
THEOPHILUS LINDSEY

Published by the University of Manchester at
THE UNIVERSITY PRESS (H. M. McKechnie, M.A., Secretary)
12 Lime Grove, Oxford Road, MANCHESTER

LONGMANS, GREEN & CO.
London : 39 Paternoster Row
New York : 443-449 Fourth Avenue and Thirtieth Street
Bombay : 8 Hornby Road
Calcutta : 6 Old Court House Street
Madras : 167 Mount Road

Vandrimini Sculp.t

REV.D THEOPHILUS LINDSEY, M.A.

LETTERS OF
THEOPHILUS LINDSEY

BY

H. McLACHLAN, M.A., D.D.

LECTURER IN HELLENISTIC GREEK IN THE UNIVERSITY OF MANCHESTER

MANCHESTER:
AT THE UNIVERSITY PRESS

LONGMANS, GREEN, & CO.
LONDON, NEW YORK, BOMBAY, ETC.

1920

CHAPTER IV

LINDSEY AND POLITICS

CHAPTER V

LINDSEY AND HIS CONTEMPORARIES

ILLUSTRATION

Frontispiece—Rev. Theophilus Lindsey, M.A., after Vandrimini.

LETTERS OF
THEOPHILUS LINDSEY

BY

H. McLACHLAN, M.A., D.D.

LECTURER IN HELLENISTIC GREEK IN THE UNIVERSITY OF MANCHESTER

MANCHESTER:

AT THE UNIVERSITY PRESS

LONGMANS, GREEN, & CO.

LONDON, NEW YORK, BOMBAY, ETC.

1920

PUBLICATIONS OF THE UNIVERSITY OF MANCHESTER

No. CXXXIV

SYNOPSIS

INTRODUCTION

CHAPTER I

LINDSEY AS A LETTER-WRITER

CHAPTER II

LINDSEY IN HIS LETTERS

CHAPTER III

LINDSEY AND ECCLESIASTICAL REFORM

CHAPTER IV

LINDSEY AND POLITICS

CHAPTER V

LINDSEY AND HIS CONTEMPORARIES

ILLUSTRATION

Frontispiece—Rev. Theophilus Lindsey, M.A., after Vandrimini.

INTRODUCTION

THEOPHILUS LINDSEY, the writer of the following letters, was born at Middlewich in Cheshire, June 20, 1723. His father, Robert Lindsey, by trade a mercer, was descended from an ancient Scottish family. His mother, whose maiden name was Spencer, was a distant relative of the Marlboroughs, and before her marriage had lived for more than twenty years in the family of Frances, Countess of Huntingdon. From Theophilus, Earl of Huntingdon, the son of this lady and his godfather, Lindsey derived his baptismal name. This connection brought him into close relations with Selina Hastings, the famous Countess of Huntingdon, the friend and patroness of George Whitefield. Fifteen years after his secession from the Established Church Lindsey and his wife called upon Lady Huntingdon at Talgarth in Wales, and, as he informed a friend, were " received graciously as usual." To the patronage of Lady Betsy and Lady Ann Hastings, his mother's friends, Lindsey owed his early education. From a school in Cheshire he went to the Leeds Grammar School, and thence to St. John's College, Cambridge (May 21, 1741), in the eighteenth year of his age. Here his sober character and academical attainments won for him the position of tutor to the grandson of Dr. Reynolds, Bishop of Lincoln, and a friendship was formed with his pupil which proved to be lifelong. In April 1747 Lindsey was elected a Fellow of St. John's College, and after ordination by Dr. Gibson, Bishop of London, was presented to a chapel in Spital Square. Soon afterwards he was appointed chaplain to Francis, Earl of Huntingdon, the nephew of Lady Ann Hastings, and, a little later, presented by the Earl of Northumberland to the rectory of Kirkby Whiske in the North Riding of Yorkshire. Here he made the acquaintance of Archdeacon Blackburne, whose step-daughter, Hannah Elsworth, he married in 1760. After three years in Yorkshire he received from his friend the Earl of Huntingdon the living of Piddleton in Dorset. Letters to Lindsey from his noble friends show how far a man of his abilities might have gone in the Church with the aid of such influential patrons. In the year 1762 the Duke of Northumberland was appointed Lord-Lieutenant of Ireland, and offered Lindsey the post of chaplain. This offer Lindsey declined in order that he might be near his father-in-law, and in July of the same year he accepted the living of Catterick in Yorkshire. Here he laboured for ten years with great acceptance. In the words of Mrs. Cappe, the daughter of the previous incumbent, " It was the constant subject of his thoughts in what way he could most effectually benefit the people committed to his care, whether in their temporal or eternal interests. And to this end a plan of great frugality was adopted by himself and Mrs. Lindsey, that they might have the power of distributing books in aid of personal instruction ; of giving medicines to the sick, and food to those who were ready to perish with hunger." At Catterick Lindsey established, in 1765, the first Sunday School in England actually so called.[1]

At the house of Archdeacon Blackburne, Lindsey met the Rev. William Turner of Wakefield and Dr. Priestley, then settled at Leeds, who became his intimate friends and constant correspondents. In 1773 Lindsey resigned his living in consequence of his adoption of Unitarian opinions. His subsequent movements, the objects of his interests, and his personal characteristics may be learnt from his letters. Lindsey's life—that of a scholar and preacher—is almost devoid of incident, save in so far as he was associated with the various ecclesiastical and political movements of the second half of the eighteenth century, which bulk so large in his correspondence. His sermons and theological writings, though widely read in his own day, made no great contribution to learning, doctrinal or historical, and have never been reprinted. The impression which the man made upon his contemporaries by his self-sacrifice, sincerity, and devotion to truth was voiced by some who differed from him in theological doctrine. Job Orton, one time assistant and confidential friend of Doddridge, said of him, " Were I to publish an account of silenced and ejected ministers, I should be strongly tempted to insert Mr. Lindsey in the list which he mentions in his *Apology* with so much veneration.

[1] Overton and Rolton, *The English Church*, vii. p. 300.

He certainly deserves as much respect and honour as
any of them for the part he has acted. Perhaps few of
them exceeded him in learning and piety. I venerate
him as I would any of your confessors. As to his particular sentiments, they are nothing to me. An honest,
pious man, who makes a sacrifice to truth and conscience
as he has done, is a glorious character, and deserves the
respect, esteem, and veneration of every true Christian."

CHAPTER I

LINDSEY AS A LETTER-WRITER

THE letter has been defined by Deissmann as "a confidential conversation." The definition, like many German doctrines, is partly true. As applied by its author to the writings of Paul the Apostle, it is misleading and inadequate, as a study of the Epistle to the Romans fully proves. But it is the truth in the definition which lends to epistolary literature its charm and interest.

Garrick described Goldsmith as one who "wrote like an angel and talked like poor Poll." Though the great Irishman was not exactly "an inspired idiot," as Horace Walpole called him, and his letters are amongst the most graphic and moving of human documents, it is certainly the case that there have been authors whose "confidential conversations" contribute nothing to their reputation. Theophilus Lindsey was not a man of this kind, and all the interest attaches to his letters that belongs to one who lived in the golden age of letter-writing—a cultured and pious minister, who broke fresh ground in Nonconformist history, and whose friends included many of the best-known figures of the eighteenth century.

By means of his letters we add greatly to our knowledge of the man and his work, for, as a recent historian of biography has observed, " Letters have come to be recognised as amongst the most effective aids to the production of the ideal type of biography." Besides, as James Howell, the author of *Familiar Letters*, said, writing as early as 1645 :

> " Letters may more than history enclose,
>   They knowledge can unto our souls display
>   By a more gentle and familiar way."

Theophilus Lindsey, the " father of Unitarian Church-manship," as he has been called, was a great letter-writer in the sense, at least, that for many years he conducted a voluminous correspondence with many friends and acquaintances. Of these, first in order of time and importance was Joseph Priestley, whose letters to Lindsey from June 5, 1769, to January 16, 1804, cover a period of nearly thirty-five years, from their introduction to each other by Archdeacon Blackburne at Richmond, Yorks, up to three weeks before Priestley's death at Northumberland, U.S.A. These letters were printed in Rutt's edition of the *Theological and Miscellaneous Works of Priestley* in 1831. With William Turner of Wake-field (1714–1794), introduced to Lindsey at the same time as Priestley, and with his son of the same name of Newcastle (1761–1859), Lindsey was in regular cor-respondence for thirty years. The lives of both men are included in the *Dictionary of National Biography*. With William Tayleur of Shrewsbury (1713–1796) Lindsey corresponded for twenty-one years, from August 4, 1775, until the death of his correspondent, May 6, 1796, though the two men did not meet until letters had been exchanged for no less than eight years. Belsham [1] has a

---

[1] *Life of Lindsey*, pp. 137-41.

brief notice of Tayleur, who was one of Priestley's greatest benefactors, and to whom he dedicated his *Letters to a Philosophical Unbeliever*. In a letter to W. Turner, sen. (September 1, 1783), written immediately after a visit to Shrewsbury, Lindsey thus describes Tayleur :

" He was educated at Westminster, and went off Captain of the school to Christ Church, Oxford, where he resided as Student or Fellow seven years, a hard and real student all the while ; thence to the Temple for nearly as long a space. But an elder brother then dying, and the family estate coming to him, he married the late Sir Rowland Hill's sister, and settled at Shrewsbury. . . . A strict Unitarian . . . some years past, when he could no longer attend the Trinitarian worship of the Church of England, and could not, through long association, join with edification in extemporary prayer, he had service for many Sundays in his own house. . . ."

In Lindsey's extant letters are included extracts of communications from forty-eight persons in the British Isles and America. These included men of all sorts and conditions, from an unnamed Tanner of Selby, Yorks, and a Mr. Hinton, ironmonger of Oxford, to Dr. Dalrymple, one time Moderator of the Scottish General Assembly, eulogised by Burns for his piety, but suspected of unsound views on the Trinity, and Edmund Law, Bishop of Carlisle, philosopher, theologian, and latitudinarian.

Of this mass of correspondence comparatively little has appeared in print. Belsham made some use of the Turner letters in his *Memoirs of Lindsey*, and gave a few extracts from letters to John Jebb, a Cambridge scholar, afterwards a theological and political writer, who followed Lindsey out of the Church of England. Rutt, in his

Life and Correspondence of Priestley, gives letters from Lindsey to Priestley and others, and Christopher Wyvill includes two letters addressed to himself in his *Political Papers*. More recently the Rev. Alexander Gordon transcribed a few letters addressed to Tayleur in the *Christian Life* (1877–78).

In 1865 Henry A. Bright of Liverpool presented to the Unitarian Home Missionary College two bound volumes of MS. letters of Theophilus Lindsey. These, addressed for the most part to Tayleur, have never been published. A few more are contained in the letters of Tayleur (August 5, 1775–July 26, 1792), recently acquired by the institution named. The two collections, together with the Turner Letters now in the Dr. Williams' Library, London, provide materials and an incentive for a fresh study of Lindsey and his times.

In form, Lindsey is orthodox as letter-writer, employing the elaborate formulæ current in the epistolary literature of the eighteenth century, opening his letters with such courtly phraseology as " Dear and much honoured Sir," or " Dear Sir, and my justly esteemed Friend," and subscribing himself " I am, with sincere respect and esteem, Dear Sir, Your truly obliged and affectionate servant." With more intimate friends like Priestley there was naturally less formality, though never anything like familiarity. Now and again he refers to his correspondent in the third person, apparently from a sense of propriety.

After a year's correspondence, Tayleur sent his good wishes to Mrs. Lindsey, whereupon her husband observes, " My wife desires to present her due respects, and to say how much she thinks herself honoured by your obliging notice and naming of her." From this time on, the due respects of Mrs. Lindsey are seldom wanting. A couple of letters from that lady herself to Tayleur (September 1776), during an illness of her husband, were deemed worthy of preservation by their recipient.

The letters of Lindsey often run to a great length, some addressed to Tayleur containing as many as 1250 words. He employed at least four seals : one, a warrior with shield ; a second, a shield of arms ; a third, a small head of Cicero ; and a fourth, a small head of Cæsar. Many of the letters are franked, and the donors of the franks, in several cases, are named in the epistles, thus affording some evidence of the number of Members of Parliament whom Lindsey counted among his friends. But he did not grudge paying postage in order to converse with his friends, and begs W. Turner, sen., to remember that postage is no matter of consideration with him, and that he only uses franks because they fall in his way.

A letter to Tayleur (October 4, 1783), written on the blank page of a circular announcing the formation of a Society for Promoting the Knowledge of the Scriptures, gives a full account of its objects and a list of the first members. Two years later, a letter to W. Turner and another to Tayleur (December 5, 1785) are written on the blank pages of a curious circular addressed to the members of the Society, bearing the autograph signature of the secretary, John Disney, Lindsey's brother-in-law and colleague at Essex Street Chapel. The circular, unlike such communications in general, announces that " the money in the Treasurer's hands would probably be sufficient for the current expenses of one year, commencing from the first day of January next. It was therefore resolved to forbear to receive any subscription from the members for the ensuing year, unless some un-

expected expenses should make it necessary to apply to
them for that purpose." The employment of the circulars
in question for the purpose of his correspondence may be
evidence of Lindsey's economy in the use of paper as well
as of his desire to bring the society before the notice of
his correspondents.

Occasionally the exigencies of his situation compelled
Lindsey to be brief. Thus, writing August 1, 1780,
from the residence of his brother-in-law, Flintham Hall,
near Newark, he tells Tayleur " I am forced to write in
more haste than I could wish on account of our being
seven miles from the post, and a gentleman waiting to
carry it." Another letter to the same person is undated,
closing with the words, " I am sorry to be prevented
finishing my letter, but would rather send it off so, than
not write at all."

The nature and purpose of the correspondence with
Tayleur are stated in the first letter, written a year and
four months after the opening of Essex Street Chapel, to
which Tayleur was a subscriber from the beginning :

" I shall think it an honour and a pleasure to converse
with you, sir, at a distance, and shall gladly do so on
your own terms. I intend, when I have a little leisure,
to send you some account of the state of our congregation,
and shall tell you of anything in the literary world in
theological matters worth communicating, and be happy
to be of service to you in that or in any other way "
(August 6, 1776).

Lindsey was in an exceptionally good situation for transmitting information relating to " the literary world," for he
was on intimate terms with the two chief publishers in
London, Joseph Johnson and Thomas Cadell. Johnson
was a personal friend, the publisher of all the works of

Priestley and his circle, and, as his biographer remarks, " for many years before his death the father of the book trade." [1]   It was Johnson who found the room in Essex House for Lindsey, and who made application to the Westminster Justices (April 11, 1774) for the registration of Essex Chapel as a place of dissenting worship. Lindsey describes him as " a worthy and most honest man, but incorrigibly neglectful, often to his own detriment."   Cadell, who " brought out the best books of the day," [2] was, as Lindsey told Tayleur, "one of our congregation, but values books of all kinds according to their vent " (June 12, 1787).   Four years earlier (January 7, 1783), Cadell and Tayleur had been associated as trustees in the first deed of Essex Street Chapel.   It was Cadell who published the *Decline and Fall*, and its completion was celebrated by what Gibbon called " a cheerful literary dinner at Mr. Cadell's house." [3]   Not infrequently Lindsey sends his friend at Shrewsbury, under the same cover as his letter, copies of pamphlets and tracts lately published on subjects in which both men were interested.

Speaking generally, Lindsey expresses his opinions on theological and ecclesiastical questions when writing to Tayleur, a layman, and writes more freely of politics, domestic and foreign, when addressing clerical brethren like the Turners.

Three letters of Tayleur, from a collection of epistles of the same type, disclose his predilection.   One, addressed to Lindsey (February 11, 1773), discusses Priestley's

[1] *Dictionary of National Biography*, Art. Johnson, Joseph.

[2] *Ibid.*, Art. Cadell, Thomas, the elder.

[3] *Memoirs of the Life of Edward Gibbon*, by Himself, ed. G. Birkbeck Hill, p. 229.

strikes oddly on our ear, as when he speaks of a certain
Jew named David Levi as "gotten into better bread
among his brethren by his publication against Priestley,"
or of Priestley "eating his lot with us," and "drinking
a dish of coffee with us," or, referring to a lady's con-
valescence, expresses the hope that she is "out of the
straw," or says of his wife, after an indisposition, "I bless
God she is now tolerably stout," meaning by the last
word "recovered," as Belsham renders it in a quotation
from the letter.   Once he asks pardon for "the to and
fro if not inconsistent things" which he had said.   Now
and again some saying of a favourite author is quoted,
like that of "good Mr. Henry," "Our clocks go too fast
for God's dial."   Addressing an Oxford man, "an excellent scholar both in Greek and Latin and not unskilled
in Hebrew," as he describes Tayleur in a letter to W.
Turner, sen., he does not hesitate to use words and
phrases in French, Latin, and Greek ; whilst in writing
to Turner, he indulges in a Latin note of some length,
enjoining secrecy respecting the authorship of a certain
anonymous *libellum*.   Lindsey's Greek is written without breathings or accents, and his transliteration of the
Hebrew word for God, "Aleim," betrays his acquaintance
with the system of Hebrew "unadulterated with the
Rabbinical points" associated with the name of his friend
John Parkhurst, the Hutchinsonian divine, of whose
Hebrew and Greek lexicons he speaks in high terms.
(Letter to Tayleur, September 22, 1784.)

   An indication of the politics of the period, and of the
liberal ideas of Lindsey and his circle, is afforded by the
treatment of his letters by the authorities :

   "I would have written to you before, but had no good
heart to it, on being told from various parts that the letters

of Dissenters, particularly Unitarians, were very commonly inspected at the Post Office. Not that this was a circumstance that gave me any apprehension on account of anything I might say to any one, but it is not pleasant to be the subject of impertinent curiosity and remarks." (Letter to Tayleur, February 8, 1793.)

Of Lindsey's style little need be said. A certain power of description may be seen, as in his reports of proceedings in the House of Commons, and a careful avoidance of exaggeration and hyperbole, as in his allusions to movements and affairs with which he was not in complete sympathy. The structure of his sentences is not always simple, and the meaning does not plainly lie on the surface. There are some signs of haste in composition. The letters are avowedly written for private reading, and lack anything like literary polish. It is perhaps equally characteristic of the man and of the period in which he lived, that in all his letters there is not so much as a single allusion to the moods and mysteries of nature, though many were written in the spring and summer seasons from the heart of the country. Lindsey contents himself with an occasional prosaic mention of the vagaries of the climate. The letters are of value only as an index to the character, interests, and pursuits of the writer, and as throwing light upon the various religious and political controversies of the age in which he lived.

CHAPTER II

LINDSEY IN HIS LETTERS

A few details of Lindsey's life, not elsewhere noted, come before us in his letters. Belsham speaks of his attendance as a youth "at a school in the neighbourhood of Middlewich," Cheshire. In a letter to W. Turner, sen. (November 11, 1771), Lindsey refers to the time when he was at school at "Rosthern near Knutsford to learn accounts for a while," and more than sixteen years later (letter to W. Turner, jun., February 4, 1788), he again mentions having been at a private school at Rosthern in Cheshire, where he went to learn accounts before he went to Cambridge, and where "there was a young man, a Peter Holland, a Dissenter," whom Lindsey "took a liking to," whose niece became the wife of his correspondent. Peter Holland, afterwards a medical practitioner at Knutsford, was the father of Sir Peter Holland, the medical attendant of the Princess of Wales, later the unfortunate Queen Caroline. His first wife was an aunt of Mrs. Gaskell the novelist, who sketched William Turner of Newcastle in "the good Mr. Benson" of *Ruth*.

Of Lindsey's habits of life his letters afford many a glimpse. He frequently entertained his visitors to breakfast. One—a Mr. Wood—travelled from Walthamstow to Essex Street on a Monday (September 2, 1784), nearly eight miles, for this purpose. The visitor, it may be assumed, was an early riser, and Lindsey himself not wont to make too much of "the parson's holiday." Occasionally Lindsey went out to breakfast. "One morning this week," he writes (February 8, 1791), when in the sixty-eighth year of his age, "I breakfasted in Downing Street, Westminster, with Mr. James Martin, member for Tewkesbury, at his desire." On another occasion he breakfasted, in the company of Priestley, with a family of Jews. "The repast," we learn, "did not continue long," but the conversation went on for an hour and a half without any pause, and it was always with difficulty, and sometimes not without vehemence, that Dr. Priestley could get to put in a word." . . . "We are to meet some Jews of still higher rank at the house of one of them to-morrow morning." (Letter to Tayleur, May 6, 1788.)

Unlike his great contemporary Samuel Johnson, Lindsey was no tea-drinker. After sitting in the House of Commons listening to the debate on the Feathers Tavern Petition with Drs. Price, Priestley, Chambers, and Mr. Ratcliff, he says, "We all drank tea afterwards at a coffee house." (Letter to W. Turner, sen., May 5, 1774.) But writing later to Tayleur (March 2, 1779), he observes, after stating that all his life he had been troubled with headaches and nervous insomnia, "I am rather better since I have quitted the use of Chinese teas." Apparently Lindsey kept his pledge, for eleven years afterwards he thus advises W. Turner, jun. (May 2, 1790), "With respect to the regimen of your diet for the future, I would proscribe the use of tea entirely, having found benefit myself by leaving it off, and many younger persons than you being delivered from many ugly sensations by refraining from it, which they know not how to account for."

Lindsey's preference for the simple life seems to be reflected in two allusions to contemporaries, one a famous London physician, another an eminent politician lately dead, who, three years earlier, had carried in the Commons the famous resolution that " the influence of the crown has increased, is increasing, and ought to be diminished."

" Dr. Wallis is at Exmouth for the benefit of the mild air of our Western coasts. He looks well, but too fat and full, and must beware of the snares of the daily pontifical meals to which he is exposed at his own and others' tables " . . . " the late Mr. Dunning, Lord Ashburton, had indeed been very intemperate in other respects, but was supposed to have hurt himself exceedingly this May. I know a club of Batchelor Counsellors whose ordinary for eating only at the Tavern each day is one Guinea per head." (Letter to W. Turner, sen., November 6, 1783.)

The closing sentence of a letter to Tayleur (March 1, 1788) illustrates the simplicity of Lindsey's character :

" I may tell you, my friend, that I have long ago resolved not to put out to interest any savings arising from my annual income, as I think I can make a better use of them."

Like many clergymen of an older generation, Lindsey was a respectable horseman, and frequently refers to his riding. A fall from his horse left him " disabled in the use of the right hand," so that for a time he was unable to answer his correspondence (November 8, 1777), but he did not abandon his exercises. " I drink asses' milk every morning," he tells Tayleur (August 21, 1784), " and have been able to be on horseback every day but one for some years." As a busy and studious man, he sometimes grudged the time thus spent. "These rustications, I believe, are serviceable to my health, as during them I endeavour to be much on horseback, but they are terrible consumers of time, which I can ill spare, as it breaks in upon many things." He kept his saddle, however, until he was far advanced in years, and when past seventy spent "eight days at Coatham by the seaside, when I had an opportunity of riding on the sands and about the country every day." (Letter to W. Turner, jun., September 9, 1793.) The problem of meeting all the demands upon his time and energies often troubled Lindsey, and a note in one of his letters shows in what direction he spared himself. "I may say to you, Sir, we are obliged to be much in reserve with respect to making visits to preserve a moment to oneself. The unavoidable avocations I have, when the Town is full, are not to be told." (Letter to Tayleur, December 20, 1781.) This confession evoked a gentle remonstrance, and a little later Lindsey returns to the subject—"though I would say that we do not deal in visits, except to a very few intimate friends, I omit no opportunity of seeing any that belong to us where it may be done, and is likely to be of any use." (Letter to Tayleur, March 30, 1782.)

Lindsey was also a club-man, and one who, by his own account, did not always go home early.

"I write this," he tells Tayleur, "at a friend's in the city where I am dining, and thence to go to a fortnight club, where I meet Dr. Price, Dr. Kippis, Mr. Lee, the counsellor at Lincoln's Inn, and many other worthies; and my wife, knowing that I should not return till late at night, has sent me your favour, which came by the post after I had left home."

This club is probably to be identified with that which " met at the London Coffee House, Ludgate Hill," and consisted of Dr. Franklin, Mr. Canton, Dr. Kippis, Dr. Shipley, the Bishop of St. Asaph, " and other philosophical gentlemen." Lindsey was a member, too, of the famous Revolution Club, and several times records his attendance at its meetings.

" July reminds me of the 14th, when the anniversary of the French Revolution is proposed to be celebrated at the Crown and Anchor near us, where I was the last year and intend this." (Letter to Tayleur, June 27, 1791.)

He describes the event eighteen days later to the same friend :

" Everything passed off in the way that every friend to the meeting could desire.   About 500 were in the room we dined in, *i.e.* Mr. Belsham, Mr. Rowe and your honourable servant, for we contrived to sit together. About 200 in an adjoining room.   The toasts I enclose."

Even in his seventy-eighth year, he speaks of meeting a friend " at dinner at Mr. Sergt. Heywood's, and we all went together to our club." (Letter to John Rowe, January 28, 1801.)

Despite his connection with the zealous spirits who foregathered at the Crown and Anchor, the Essex Street minister was a conspicuously mild man.   Augustus Toplady, the celebrated Calvinist Methodist preacher, said of him after hearing him preach, " He seems to be a man of much personal modesty and diffidence, and, I verily believe, acts upon principle, but he has no popular talents. He is no more qualified to figure as the head of a party than I am to take the command of the navy."   Lindsey's mild temperament is betrayed in many a phrase of his letters, and, incidentally, his methods of composition are disclosed. When submitting his *Apology for Resigning the Living at Catterick* in MS. to his friend at Wakefield, he observes :

" I beg you will particularly mark any expression of sentiment that savoureth of pride, or obstinacy, or contempt of others' opinions, or that is deficient in a proper and humble sense of myself." (June 21, 1773.)

Similarly, speaking of the forthcoming publication of his *Historical Review*, the first draft of which contained a severe censure of Socinus for his treatment of Francis David, he informs Tayleur (October 30, 1781) :

" One thing I had in my mind to have mentioned ; I mean lest in the title of the intended preliminary discourse, there should be anything savouring not of the Christian spirit against those Unitarians that have hurt the cause they ought to promote. And therefore I shall alter the title. I am warm in my opinion at first against the things I dislike, particularly in the company of friends, but I always cool on reflection, and blame myself. And we ought always to use moderation, never in speaking the truth, but always in our reflections on others and their conduct."

The manner, hardly less than the matter, of Gibbon's writing offended Lindsey :

" Mr. Gibbon's answer to Davis is written with smothered resentment, which shows he is hurt, which, I think, he hardly would be, if conscious of having acted fairly and used no mean arts. And though he pretends not to love polemics, and is full of affectation upon the subject, he seems to me to love scolding as much as any of the oyster-men at Billingsgate." (Letter to W. Turner, sen., February 1779.)

In the same strain, alluding to his work, *The Catechist*, he again contrasts the spirit he cultivates with that of Gibbon :

"The present preface will be altered somewhat. I have treated Gibbon a little in the same way that he treats Christians and their cause ; which, on further thoughts, I think not quite grave enough for me, though his artifice cannot be too much exposed." (Letter to Tayleur, June 4, 1781.)

A month later he expresses satisfaction with the emendation, and adds :

"There never was a more industrious or more artful adversary to Divine Revelation than our Historian, and not many of more ability."   (Letter to Tayleur.)

Though frequently involved in controversy, Lindsey never enjoyed it :

"If I live, I hope sometime to have done with controversy.   In the meantime I watch myself.   There are one or two things in the preface to the examination of Robinson which I could wish unsaid."   (Letter to Tayleur, September 1, 1787.)

His published works afford no indication of Lindsey's sense of humour such as his letters provide.   He hits off with gentle irony the weakness of learned dons, as when in reference to the pending prosecution of William Frend for heresy, he says :

"The heads at Cambridge have hitherto done nothing but growl.   They are indeed sufficiently taken up with their adulation of the young prince, and the Bill for paving the town."   (Letter to Tayleur, May 6, 1788.)

He can tell a good story.   Speaking of John Garnet, one of Bishop Clayton's adversaries, who succeeded him in the bishopric of Clogher, he says :

" It is said that soon after he was advanced to the bishopric, a gentleman who was a friend of Bp. Clayton, preaching before him took for his text that passage, ' Hast thou killed and also taken possession ? '   No mitred head was more fond of the purple.   A pompous, talking man, he has been of late years on the Continent—always in purple and in his pontificalibus.   He was admitted in them to hear some exercises in the Sorbonne.   I saw him several times in the streets and public places in London in purple.   And so much for John Garnet."   (Letter to W. Turner, sen.)

Another anecdote relating to an American bishop also exhibits Lindsey's contempt for pomp and pride :

" The Dr. told me an anecdote relating to the new Bp. Seabury.   I hope it will have good consequences in warning the American to take care of the Bishop's foot. At their Commencement, or general meeting, at the College in Connecticut, Bp. Seabury sent word to Dr. Stiles, a correspondent of Dr. Price's, the President of the College, signifying his intention of being there, and his expectation of a proper distinction being paid him, on having a place elevated above the rest.   To this Dr. Stiles sent a civil, obliging answer, but one thing he could tell him, that if he came, he would meet 191 as good Bishops as himself."   (Letter to Tayleur, December 5, 1785.)

" The Bishop's foot " is a Yorkshire phrase.   Burnt milk is said to have had " the bishop's foot " in it.   Mrs. Gaskell in *Sylvia's Lovers*, where the scene is laid in Whitby, makes one of her characters say, " Have an eye on the milk and see it does not bile o'er, for she canna stomach it if it is bishopped e'er so little."

In a letter written in his seventy-fifth year, Lindsey reports with some relish a pun made by his wife about two students, one of whom, a friend of William Hazlitt, afterwards became the father of an eminent Unitarian divine :

" Mr. Martin, that was at Yarmouth, is in town attending a course of chemical lectures, he and your Mr. Wicksteed, both lodging together at a place called Maze Pond in the Borough, to be near St. Thomas' Hospital, where the lectures are read.   My wife remarks that the place of their abode is ominous, both the students being in a sad maze."   (Letter to John Rowe, November 27, 1797.)

Lindsey and his Chapel

The opening of Essex Street Chapel, London—the first avowedly Unitarian place of worship in England—and the events that led up to it, are described in some detail in the correspondence of Lindsey.   He mentions the proposal (December 19, 1773) that he should settle at the Octagon Chapel, Liverpool, on leaving Catterick, made independently by Archdeacon Blackburne and William Turner of Wakefield.   In a letter to the latter Lindsey observes :

" I could wish, and I think it my duty to be instrumental in bringing those who are now in the darkness in which I was bred up to the acknowledgement and worship of the One True God, through the mediation and according to the true doctrine of our Saviour Christ, rather than attach myself to those who are already emancipated from that darkness.   And we are willing to expend what little we have for that end for a year or two in Town, and make the trial.   Should it fail, I should be glad to be useful in any congregation where the worship of the true God is allowed and professed."

Upon his arrival in London he writes to W. Turner, sen. (February 9, 1774):

" Dr. Priestley is indefatigable in his endeavours, and to him, Dr. Price and other friends of theirs will it be owing that the matter is brought to bear at last. They kindly offer by the subscription of their friends to indemnify me in the first onset. If it be of God, as I trust, it will succeed. But should it fail, some good, I shall well persuade myself, will result, and others will easier take it up and proceed better. I desire the help of your prayers for illumination and always."

Another overture made to Lindsey at this time has not hitherto been noticed. Addressing his friend at Wakefield, he says (March 17, 1774):

" I must now acknowledge another instance of your friendship to me in the very friendly enquiry after me, and the genteel offer by your friend Holland from Dr. Percival. At present I am engaged in another pursuit which I cannot desert. But, besides this, though I made some little progress in the mathematics at Cambridge, I have so entirely neglected those studies since that it would not be easy for me to resume them."

Dr. Thomas Percival (1740–1804), a pupil of Warrington Academy, was the virtual founder of the Manchester Literary and Philosophical Society. He was greatly interested in his *alma mater*, and in its successor the Manchester Academy. The allusion by Lindsey is almost certainly to a possible appointment on the staff of the Warrington Academy, for in 1774 George Walker resigned the mathematical chair there and accepted a call to the ministry of the High Pavement Chapel, Nottingham. A third offer made to Lindsey at this time was that of the Earl of Huntingdon, son of the celebrated

Countess. Though himself an unbeliever, he wrote an appreciation of Lindsey's integrity, and declared his readiness to appoint him his librarian at a handsome salary. Lindsey, however, was bent on delivering his message. The efforts of Priestley, Price, John Lee and others to provide him an opening in London ultimately proved successful :

" After long search we have at last met with a room that may do for a chapel, though we should have been more glad of one of the many that have formerly been such but are now turned into warehouses. . . . The room we have taken is in Essex House, Essex Street, Strand, near the Temple." (Letter to W. Turner, sen., March 19, 1774.)

It was intimated to Lindsey that the civil authorities might frustrate his design.

" Two of the Commons House have desired to see me, and to divert me from a design which will turn that general compassion shown towards me into open hostility and hatred." (Letter to John Jebb, February 28, 1774.)

The chapel, with accommodation for three hundred persons, was opened April 17, 1774. For some time a Government agent attended the services, but ceased to do so upon failing to discover that the preaching of Unitarian doctrine was not another name for obnoxious political propaganda. In a series of letters to his friends, Lindsey describes the progress of the new society :

" The want of an Unitarian church with a precomposed form of prayer in this great city has appeared in several instances since the chapel in Essex Street was opened. Not that I look for a very great number. These are not times for it. I am led the more to say this, when I see the comparative smallness that attend on the preaching of so excellent and eminent a person as Dr. Price, though he has a larger number in the summer than in the winter. . . . We have about thirty names on the list of our Society as members. . . . I mention this, not as if I had any doubt of a sufficient provision for myself, but that you may know in a general way the whole of our state ; because I find from Miss Harrison, who had her information from Richmond, that it is there said I have already an establishment of four hundred pounds a year, and that I knew what a good exchange I should make when I left Catterick. It is here spread about and believed by many, that my wife's uncle, at our quitting Catterick, settled £200 a year on me, though he has never seen us, nor admitted us even to write a letter to him from that time to this. I believe, with Mr. Shore's and his friend's benefaction, and that of other friends, I have received upwards of four hundred pounds ; but upwards of two hundreds of this was given purely to indemnify me for the expenses of fitting up the chapel : its rent—fifty pounds a year—the Clerk's wages, etc. I am a little sorry I have blotted so much paper and taken up so much of your time on such a subject, but I was desirous you should be acquainted with it. And, as I have hitherto done, I hope to keep my hands and heart clean of all mercenary views, though I cannot hinder others imputing them to me." (Letter to W. Turner, sen., June 13, 1774.)

Miss Catherine Harrison, mentioned above, was the daughter of Lindsey's predecessor at Catterick, and afterwards became the wife of the Rev. Newcome Cappe, minister of St. Saviourgate Chapel, York. In a letter to W. Turner, sen. (June 26, 1774), she described Lindsey's lodgings at 21 Featherstone Buildings, Holborn, as " close, inconvenient, and expensive." In her *Memoirs* (1822) Mrs. Cappe gives a more detailed picture of the conditions under which Lindsey for four and a half years lived.

The Lindseys had been driven to sell " the plate which they had brought with them to London to purchase necessaries for present subsistence." [1]

" In the following May (1774), I realised the hope I had many months indulged, of visiting Mr. and Mrs. Lindsey, in London. I found them in a small lodging, upon the ground-floor of a house in Featherstone Buildings, Holborn ; the first floor was occupied by more affluent lodgers, and I had an apartment up two pairs of stairs, in the pilgrim style. Mr. Lindsey had no place for the remnant of his library (most of his books he had been compelled to sell before coming to London) but a small closet through the bedchamber, which served at once for his study, and for their store-room and cellar. The books were piled upon each other, and as there was no room for a chair or table, were so contrived as that part of them should serve as a seat, and the other part as a writing-desk. Under all these circumstances, Mr. L. was cheerful, easy, and contented : the people of the house dressed their victuals, of which a very small portion sufficed." [2]

It was in this humble lodging that Priestley declared he passed some of the most pleasing hours of his life, when, in consequence of living with Lord Shelburne, he wintered in London.

The attempt of Lindsey to secure a colleague in the ministry met with no success for a considerable period. He did not desire " a liberal Dissenter," and " could not but be contented with a Unitarian, who believed it idolatrous to worship, or pray to, any but the Father." (Letter to Tayleur, February 3, 1781.) His friend John Jebb declined the invitation, when in 1776 he left

---

[1] Belsham, *Memoirs of Lindsey*, p. 98.
[2] Cappe, *Memoirs*, p. 176.

Cambridge ; and on the advice of his cousin, Sir Richard
Jebb, he took up the study of medicine.   In April 1778
William Robertson, D.D., Master of the Wolverhampton
Grammar School, who had left the Church fourteen
years earlier, agreed to become Lindsey's colleague, but
when threatened with prosecution for teaching without
a licence, resolved to stay where he was and meet it.   As
a matter of fact no proceedings were taken against him.
Next year Tayleur suggested to his friend, Paul H. Maty,
who had recently broken with the Church, and was at
this time assistant librarian in the British Museum and
foreign secretary of the Royal Society.   The appointment
is discussed at some length two years later :

" From the very first year of my being placed there
with some prospect of going forwards, I have diligently
sought a colleague, but, for obvious reasons, one out of
the Church of England.   One, two, three ; two of whom
I could have wished, and made every offer I could, did
not thus prefer to engage or go on in the character of
gospel Ministers, and the third the same, though I
made him no proposal for I had no time.   Mr. Maty
would not, I believe, be averse to the office, for he is a
worthy man, but he has declared his scruples to preach
for one that believes not the pre-existence.   For near
two years, through Mr. Toulmin, I have been laying
out for a worthy friend who quitted officiating in the
Church, but, alas, about a year ago, renewed it to assist
a brother and oblige his family, yet not approving what
he did."   (Letter to Tayleur, February 3, 1781.)

The clergyman in question was Charles Toogood,
and in another communication to Tayleur (May 3,
1781), Lindsey transcribes his letter, written from Sher-
borne, declining the invitation.   In November 1782,
the Rev. John Disney, a friend and brother-in-law of

Lindsey, resigned his living, and intimated his willingness to accept the office. His settlement in London, his literary labours, and succession to Lindsey upon his retirement, are all described in Lindsey's letters. It is interesting to notice that Lindsey had never heard Disney preach when he asked him to become his colleague.

" I have the satisfaction of acquainting you that Dr. Disney, who married my wife's sister, has been this day with the Bp. of Lincoln to acquaint him of his intended resignation of the livings of Swinderby and Panton in Lincolnshire. . . . On Sunday he is to preach to our congregation, and I hope he will prove acceptable to them. I never heard him preach, but I have a good hope he will be useful in that capacity, and by his private study and application recommend himself more and more. . . . After he has preached here he goes back to Swinderby, and hopes to be able to settle all his matters and come up with his family about the beginning of the new year."

In the year 1777 we read of structural alterations at Essex House, of the purchase of the premises, and of a new chapel on the site :

" The temporary chapel we hope will make a habitation for the minister, being under the other, and though rather low, we hope will not be unwholesome." (Letter to Tayleur, September 4, 1777.)

Three months later Lindsey informs the same correspondent :

" I had given out Sunday next for the day of our reassembling in our temporary chapel at Essex House, but the taking down the front wall will retard our meeting. I am assured by the Surveyor, however, that he will be ready for us on Sunday the 25th ; and I have accordingly privately circulated the notice for that day. Some were for mentioning our secession in the public prints, and also to advertise the day of our meeting again ; but everything of that kind that might be construed into a design to invite or draw a crowd has from the first been uniformly avoided." (Letter, September 4, 1777.)

The new chapel was not opened until March 29, 1778. Three days later Lindsey describes the opening in a letter to Tayleur :

" I am now to acquaint with what will give you much satisfaction—that our new chapel was opened on Sunday last for the first time. To avoid a crowd or disturbance, we kept it as private as we could, and I preached to our wonted congregation. The whole passed very well ; every one was pleased with the room ; it turned out much better to speak in than was expected on account of the large dome by which it is lighted, and some were satisfied with the preacher, for he was at the time and has been since importuned to print the sermon, and accordingly sends it to press to-morrow."

One reason for the caution and privacy of Lindsey's advocacy of Unitarian worship may be found in the fact that such worship was still liable to certain penalties— Unitarians being excluded from the Toleration Act of 1689, and the Act to relieve persons who impugn the doctrine of the Holy Trinity from the possible consequences of their action not being passed until 1813. It was a case of letting sleeping dogs lie. Lindsey's sermon, from John iv. 23, 24, was a defence of Unitarian worship. Incidentally, the preacher disclaimed anything like sacerdotalism, and indicated the place of reason in the interpretation of scripture. Three months later we learn :

" The house is not yet all of it habitable, but after being cooped up four years and a half in lodgings, crowded with other guests, it is a great refreshment to have one or two cool rooms to ourselves at the hot season." (Letter to Tayleur.)

Even Lindsey's house beneath the chapel had its disadvantages, for, when apologising for his reception of a lady visitor, he tells Tayleur (April 20, 1784):

"Our room was so crowded, as it commonly is before and after Chapel, that we could not ask her to sit down."

And, in speaking of his wife's mother coming to reside at Richmond, he adds :

"We are so situated that we have not a bed to offer anyone, though our house makes a splendid appearance." (Letter to Tayleur, September 1, 1787.)

The attendance of various notables upon Lindsey's ministry is remarked by Belsham, including Sir George Saville, M.P. for Yorkshire, a stalwart defender of Dissent in the House of Commons ; Michael Dodson, an eminent barrister and a student of scripture ; Sir Thomas Brand, the benevolent treasurer of the Foundling Hospital ; Richard Kirwan, F.R.S., the President of the Royal Society in Ireland, a distinguished and eccentric savant ; John Lee, K.C., Solicitor-General and afterwards Attorney-General in the Rockingham Administration ; Mrs. Rayner, a relative of three members of the nobility, and many others. The last-named, according to Mrs. Cappe,[1] "heard of Mr. Lindsey by the following accident. Her maid one day asked her permission to go to Essex Street, where she had heard that a gentleman was going to open a room to preach a new religion. Permission was obtained, and on her return, Mrs. R., not being perfectly satisfied with the young

[1] *Memoirs*, pp. 176-7.

woman's very imperfect account, determined to call upon the gentleman herself, which she did accordingly the following morning, and upon hearing a full explanation of the object intended, and of the circumstances that had led to it, she not only gave it her most entire approbation, but became afterwards one of its greatest and most steady friends."

Introduced by Lindsey to Priestley, Mrs. Rayner also became one of the most generous patrons of the latter. To her Priestley dedicated his *History of Early Opinions concerning Christ*, and she bequeathed to him at death the sum of £2000. Her close friendship with Mr. and Mrs. Lindsey is reflected in the circumstance that, by her wish, she was interred in the same vault as they afterwards occupied.

These distinguished members of his congregation and many others are frequently mentioned in Lindsey's letters. In connection with the appearance of two such he writes :

" Since last I wrote you, we have had the accession of a new member to our society—Mr. Whitmore, member for Bridgnorth. It was after the service on Christmas Day that he came up and spoke to me, and desired to be accommodated with a pew. . . . I may also mention that the Earl of Surrey frequently attends our worship, but mixed with the crowd in the seats under the galleries. I wish anything he may hear may induce him to make a right use of the good sense and liberal principles of which he appears to be possessed, for I have sometimes been in company and converse with him." (Letter to Tayleur, June 13, 1780.)

But not all the members of the nobility who sympathised with Lindsey threw in their lot with him. We find, for example, that

"Lord Hardwicke, at our Liturgy's first coming out, expressed to some friends of mine his approbation of it. But it all ended there." (Letter to Tayleur, December 1, 1785.)

It required, indeed, some courage to attend Essex Street Chapel, and Lindsey "gently admonished" a young friend of Tayleur, Binyon by name, who had come up to town in order to study law, that he might "be ridiculed for his singularity in attending the worship of our chapel." (Letter to Tayleur, January 24, 1782.)

Lindsey's hearers did not always attend twice a day. He informs Tayleur (July 12, 1781):

"I have given notice, as was done last year in my absence, that there would be duty only in the forenoon till further notice, a thing, I guess, will be for the space of six Sundays. For what with the absence of the greater part, and the indifference of others, and unwillingness to alter their dinner hour, though we begin not till four o'clock, we have often not more than a dozen persons that belong to us, though sometimes, yet not always, a tolerable congregation of other persons. In the mornings we generally make a decent show for numbers. I did not advertise them of this without some reproof for their negligence, preaching to them on Sunday last on the subject of the Sabbath."

The temporary abandonment of the afternoon service created some apprehension in the mind of Lindsey's correspondent, to which he alludes in a later letter (September 29, 1781):

"I was myself sorry to be constrained to take such a step. But when I did it, I told them that the general negligence of many was one cause. I also took care to have the door still open in an afternoon, and our Clerk attending, to tell casual visitors that the worship was only suspended for a time.   And at resuming it, I discoursed to them on the duty of attending divine worship both parts of the Lord's Day, and the infinite detriment done to their servants, families, neighbours, by a neglect of it, as well as to themselves.   During the interval, when I went to other places in the afternoons, it was melancholy to observe how few attended.   At the Old Jewry on a fine day there were fifteen persons and three children.   Mr. White delivered a very Christian, useful sermon.   This, as I mentioned it to our people, though without specifying name or place, was most discouraging, as well as of bad omen, and like preaching to naked walls.   I remember often, in that very place, they could hardly contain the audiences, for in former days I was a hearer of Foster and Chandler."

James Foster (1697–1753) is said to have enjoyed "a degree of popularity unexampled among Protestant Dissenters." [1]   His fame is indicated by Pope's lines (*Epilogue to the Satires*, i. 132-3).

> "Let modest Foster, if he will, excel
> Ten Metropolitans in preaching well."

Samuel Chandler (1693–1766), minister of Old Jewry from 1726 until his death, was a distinguished divine and a voluminous writer.   Nathaniel White was at Old Jewry from 1766 until his death on March 3, 1783.

The attendance at afternoon service in Essex Street Chapel did not improve, and Lindsey found little consolation in the widespread indifference to public worship.

"Our Chapel is always well filled in the forenoon with foreigners, if our members are absent.   But it is far from being so in the afternoon in any part of the year for several years past.   And, such is our solitude that, had I no colleague, I should be tempted to drop the afternoon

[1] Wilson, *Dissenting Churches*, ii. p. 274.

service entirely, with this declaration and reserve—to be resumed if a competent number of the congregation would engage themselves to attend. We have the comfort, if there is any comfort in that, there are the same empty walls at the Old Jewry, Prince's Street, etc., but I cannot say that there is much satisfaction in it." (Letter to Tayleur, July 7, 1791.)

Essex Street Chapel, nevertheless, enjoyed a certain reputation, and Lindsey reports to Tayleur (November 29, 1788):

" A compliment one gentleman of our congregation of fortune paid us, of a kind little expected, at Tunbridge Wells . . . who recommended ours as the only genteel place in London for his friend to go to."

It is a singular fact that Essex Street Chapel was not licensed as a place of worship when it was opened, nor for several years afterwards. Belsham mentions the application that was made in 1774 and what happened to it, quoting a letter from Lindsey to Dr. Jebb, written on the day the licence was promised, after John Lee, K.C., had instructed the justices as to their obligation to issue the certificate. The letter concludes :

" Our certificate, it was said, should be ready next court-day. We begin, however, without it on the authority of our counsel."

It was not until ten years later that the chapel was licensed, when Dr. Horsley called attention to it in his *Letters to Dr. Priestley*. Lindsey thus refers to the matter :

" You have not perhaps seen Dr. Horsley's blustering, insolent letters to Dr. Priestley. They are very extra-ordinary in their kind, and at this time of day, and to be dated also from Fulham Palace, as if countenanced by

the Bishop, whose Chaplain he is. . . . With regard to
our Chapel, of which he gives such a representation, I
was not unmindful at its first opening of doing what the
law required, and Mr. Lee himself took the trouble to
make the motion at Hicke's Hall for Essex House being
registered as a place of Protestant Dissenting Worship in
the year 1774.   But, if this had not been done, the large
descanting which he makes use of upon such a subject
shows rather a Laudean turn of mind." (Letter to
W. Turner, sen., July 31, 1784.)

Writing a few days later to Tayleur (August 23, 1784),
the subject is discussed.

" I presume Dr. Horsley's Letters will have reached you.
You will find that the letter in which he trounces Dr.
Priestley and us at Essex House so roundly, as unpro-
tected by the laws, has given offence to his friend and
admirer, Mr. Maty. . . . I have spoken to the former
and the present Clerk of the Peace for the county of
Middlesex for a certificate of our being registered, but
have always been put off, not, I believe, out of any
motive, but mere indolence ; neither of them acting
themselves, but leaving the whole to deputies.   On Dr.
Horsley's public accusation, I renewed my requests.   The
books have been searched.   No such record appears.
But they are now searching the Minutes, and expect to
find the matter there.   And I am told that they have
lately been much importuned to search their books,
which, I imagine, was by Dr. Horsley or on his account.
I send, however, the enclosed to you to show that there
had been no neglect in this behalf."

" The enclosed " is a copy of John Lee's letter (July 12,
1784), made by Mrs. Lindsey, in which the chapel is
described as " the place for Protestant Dissenting Worship
in Essex Street," and the clerk is reminded that " it was
ordered to be registered on my motion in the year 1774

at a meeting of Quarter Sessions, at which were many Justices, and among the rest the late Lord Dudley." Soon after this the licence was obtained without any difficulty. The hesitation to issue it in the first instance was due, Belsham suggests, to the nature of the doctrine to be preached ; a matter which, Lee pointed out, was not within the purview of the licensing authorities, though, as we have seen, almost half a century was to elapse before those who attacked the doctrine of the Trinity were relieved from all penalties.

Lindsey on Preachers and Preaching

Estimated by the number and quality of his hearers, Lindsey must be regarded as a preacher of considerable attractiveness. A liberal Anglican clergyman, Christopher Wyvill, thus describes him : " As a Preacher, he was earnest and impressive ; his discourses were delivered from the heart, with a mild and affectionate warmth which touched the heart of his audience, resembling what the imagination might conceive of the Evangelist St. John, whose religion was happiness, and whose God was benevolence." Belsham remarks on the seriousness and gravity of the discourse, which he heard in Essex Street Chapel in January 1779, ten years before his conversion to Unitarianism, and the terms admirably describe the published sermons of Lindsey. Though he founded the first avowedly Unitarian chapel in England, and was frequently engaged, through the Press, in controverting the doctrinal positions of orthodox divines, Lindsey, as already stated, disliked controversy, and " pledged himself in pretty strong language not to introduce disputed points into his public discourses." [1],[2] But

---

[1] Belsham, *Memoirs of Lindsey*, p. 116.   [2] See note, p. 42.

the circumstances in which he was placed did not suffer him to abstain altogether from controversy.

" Yesterday I ventured to deviate from the idea, which you and my friends with you seemed to entertain as right, of preaching merely practical discourses, and enlarged with much earnestness on John xvii. 3. I find it was acceptable to many, and that it was even looked for, that I should sometimes treat upon the great object and principle on which our new Church is formed, in order to confirm some that are already come out, and awaken others to come out of Babylon." (Letters to Jebb, May 23, 1774.)

A later letter to Tayleur (January 13, 1780) gives the gist of a Christmas Day sermon, as ingenious as it is controversial.

" In speaking upon the subject that there was no such appointment to be observed by Christ or his apostles, or thought of by Christians of near two hundred years, and that we certainly kept it at a wrong time of year, I took occasion to say that if any asked why we commemorated the days of the birth and death of Christ, that in the present state of the Christian world, we hold it our duty to bear our testimony to what we believed to be the truth concerning our Saviour Christ, that he was not God, or the object of divine worship—for God cannot be born or die, can have no beginning or end of existence dependent on the will of another."

Politics Lindsey kept out of the pulpit, though in public and in private he never concealed his sympathy with the Whig party, his horror of the war with America, and his high hopes of the French Revolution. Writing to Tayleur (May 16, 1789), he says :

" In the affairs of our own state, as they have been conducted for near twenty years past, and especially since our disputes with America, I cannot hesitate in my own thoughts what counsels you approve or condemn, but to engage and go all lengths with any particular set of men is a very different thing. It has been my unvaried sentiment, that unless upon a very particular call indeed, a Minister of the gospel should not seek to distinguish himself by being an actor in such matters."

Speaking of his own preaching and preparation for pulpit work, he confides in his friend :

" I would also add to such a friend as you, with whom I think aloud, that every week my Sunday's preparation engages me one day at least, sometimes more. For I hardly ever preach in the mornings a sermon preached before, unless much improved, and at a very long interval. And though my worthy colleague is much liked, I continue to preach in the forenoon except on the first Sunday in the month, when Dr. Disney undertakes it, and I administer the Communion. On other days, he officiates in the afternoons. He that preaches reads the prayers also, for to me it has always appeared too Cathedral-like to make any partition here."

Lindsey's revision of the Prayer Book, as might be expected, is discussed in detail in letters to Tayleur. Of the Apostles' Creed, which he had retained in his service, he says :

" I shall not be satisfied till we have expunged it, though my sentiments are not altered with respect to the miraculous conception. But the more one reads and thinks, the very thing itself, creed, becomes odious. . . . I must inform you also that Mr. Belsham agreed with me that frequent change of posture was not perhaps a thing to be objected to, to prevent the universal languor which obtains in all Dissenting places of worship."
(February 10, 1790.)

From the next edition of his Liturgy, the Apostles'
Creed was omitted.   Writing to Tayleur with regard to
that edition, Lindsey declares :

" Many things are left in which my successor will
probably alter in a future edition, but which I judged
right to leave untouched now ; especially the king and
royal family engrossing so much particular attention and
space."   (May 10, 1793.)

At a date less than four months after the execution of
Louis XVI., in view of the feeling in this country, and
of his contemplated retirement from the ministry, Lindsey
did not deem it expedient to evince his opinion of
George III. in his public Liturgy, though it is clearly
shown in his private correspondence.   The alteration in
question was not made by Disney, who in 1802 introduced a new form of prayer of his own composition.
When contemplating a visit to his Shrewsbury friend,
Lindsey enquired " if it would be agreeable " to preach
in the chapel in High Street, adding, " In general, I do
not like preaching out of my own place.   I have always
avoided it."   (June 23, 1782.)   In a subsequent letter
he gives a further reason for his enquiry.

" I was induced to ask the question I did, because I
have found such unaccountable prejudices against those
whom they call Socinians in more than one of those who
call themselves Arians, so as hardly to allow the former
to be Christians, and to have a total reluctance to join
with them in the same worship."   (July 24, 1782.)

The last remark illustrates the observation of the
historian of *The Arian Movement in England* : " There
was no deep friendship between the Arian and the Socinian,
although each agreed that the other ought to be tolerated." [1]

[1] Colligan, p. 4.

Occasionally Lindsey was a hearer of the word, and records his impressions of various discourses to which he listened.

" Mr. Frend preached for Mr. Morgan in the afternoon without notes, as is his custom, and upon a text, as Dr. Priestley tells us, chosen only half an hour before he went into the pulpit, and spoke without hesitation much plain sense upon the subject." (Letter to W. Turner, jun., May 4, 1790.)

Evidently Priestley himself was not so ready a preacher, for Lindsey, after mentioning that an accident he had sustained made it difficult for him to conduct the services at Essex Street, adds :

" The Sunday before last was most painful, though it was Communion, and Dr. Priestley present ; it should be added also that he had come without a sermon." (Letter to Tayleur, October 15, 1791.)

None the less the pulpit utterances of Priestley frequently evoked his admiration.

" Of his sermon on November 5, friend and foe speak most favourably.   And indeed, I know not the man save himself, who could at once, at one sitting, with so much ease and perspicuity put together so much excellent sense upon the subject "   (Letter to W. Turner, jun., February 10, 1790.)

High praise is also awarded to a certain sermon of Thomas Belsham, afterwards his successor and biographer.

" On Wednesday last we heard Mr. Belsham deliver the Annual Sermon before the Governors and friends of our new College.   I have seldom been equally pleased or edified.   You will form some conjecture about it, when I tell you that in more passages than one, Dr. Priestley, Mr. Frend and myself, who sat together in the gallery of Old Jewry, could not refrain from taking out our handkerchiefs, and were particularly pleased to observe several of the youths of the College, in the gallery opposite to us, equally moved." (Letter to W. Turner, jun., May 4, 1790.)

The sermon referred to, on *The Importance of Truth, and the Duty of making an open Profession of it,* was afterwards published. It does not contain passages of an emotional character such as would seem likely to move the feelings of experienced preachers like Priestley and Lindsey, to say nothing of the students of the ill-fated Hackney Academy (1786–1796), whose successors, by their wild escapades, did so much to terminate the existence of their *alma mater*. The words of Lindsey must be understood primarily as a tribute to the personality of the preacher. Belsham, however, was a powerful pulpiteer, and further mention of his gifts, and of his manner of conducting service, is found in a letter to Tayleur.

" We went on Sunday to hear Mr. Belsham. I have always been edified and instructed under him ; never more so than at this time. He substitutes, as Dr. Priestley did, a short exposition of a portion of the scriptures for the reading of a chapter, which takes about ten or twelve minutes." (September 16, 1795.)

These expositions Belsham afterwards published. In a letter from Tunbridge Wells, where he was spending a short holiday, Lindsey speaks in a somewhat different strain of a preacher whom he heard there.

" A Baptist minister here, originally of some trade, but now in years and enjoying a tolerable competency, is preacher to a congregation consisting seldom of more than twenty or thirty. He is wholly self-taught ; has some smattering of learning, with a good deal of acuteness and readiness, and, I fancy, must acquit himself very well to the capacity of his general hearers, and would also suit others, had he not a habit of miscalling certain words, which is not likely to be cured." (Letter to Tayleur, September 20, 1790.)

Lindsey did not share the prejudices of many University men against the preaching and teaching of those who had not enjoyed an academic training. On the contrary, he recognised the need of a special type of men for work amongst the masses of his countrymen. Referring in 1790 to the Unitarian street preachers, whom Priestley saw in Manchester, he wrote :

" It will be very desirable to have their numbers increased. We want to have the common people applied to, as enough has been done, and is doing, for the learned and higher ranks."

In the same year (October 3), writing to W. Turner, jun., respecting certain criticisms of Edward Prowitt, who had been educated at the Baptist College, Bristol, and after a brief ministry at Oxford had become a Unitarian, and was at this time serving a society of Unitarian Baptists in Newcastle, Lindsey said :

" I think I saw that prejudices might operate, and perhaps the setting too high a rate upon a regular academical education."

Amongst his correspondents was a Welshman named Thomas Evans, whom, in a letter to Tayleur (June 6, 1782), he describes as

" A self-taught Unitarian in Wales, who had instructed many in the village he lived in, and brought them on so much that they were desirous and solicited assistance towards a place to assemble in. I will endeavour to serve him, and have desired to know what sum they have calculated they still want for their building."

In the training of men for the ministry, Lindsey took a deep, personal interest, and the story of Hackney College can almost be told in the language of his letters to Tayleur. Both men were members of the Committee, of which Thomas Rogers, father of Samuel Rogers the poet, was chairman. Belsham was on the staff from 1769 to the dissolution of the institution. Priestley for a time lectured on history and chemistry, and Gilbert Wakefield was classical tutor, 1790–91. From first to last Tayleur was one of its most generous supporters. John Rowe, another of Lindsey's correspondents, was one of the earliest students of the College, and amongst its *alumni* were Arthur Aitkin, the chemist; William Hazlitt, the essayist; and Charles Wellbeloved, afterwards Principal of Manchester College, York. Notwithstanding the eminence of its teachers and the ability of many of its students, the College proved a dismal failure. An ambitious building scheme involved the institution in heavy debt. The students were carried away by the revolutionary spirit of the period, and were not readily amenable to discipline, whilst Belsham's hands were too strictly tied by the committee of management. Amongst the escapades reported of the students are the entertainment of Tom Paine to a republican supper in the College, a disturbance in a theatre occasioned by the call of the students for " Ça ira," instead of " God save the King," and, most calamitous of all, the authorship of a handbill whose circulation in Birmingham led to the famous riots of July 1791. Theological errors were also rife, and

laxity of conduct not unknown.   In one case, however,
Lindsey tells Tayleur why a certain student

" was desired not to come any more to the College—
no dice, but such a habit of driving hackney coaches that
he was continually on the box."

NOTE ON PAGE 34

Lindsey's practice in preaching is illustrated in Charles Lamb's essay on
My Relations.

Speaking of his Aunt, whose favourite volumes were Thomas à Kempis
and a Roman Catholic Prayer Book, he writes : " Finding the door of the
chapel in Essex Street open one day—it was in the infancy of that heresy—
she went in, liked the sermon and the manner of worship, and frequented
it at intervals for some time after.   She came not for doctrinal points and
never missed them."

CHAPTER III

LINDSEY AND ECCLESIASTICAL REFORM

THE first reform movement with which Lindsey was actively associated was that known as the Feathers Tavern Association. The name was derived from the tavern in the Strand where the association held its meetings. Its formation was largely due to the impression made upon the liberal clergy and laity of the Church of England by Archdeacon Blackburne's *Confessional* (1st edition, May 1766), which pleaded for the abolition of subscription by clergymen save to a belief in the Scriptures as containing a revelation of the mind and will of God. Lindsey, by personal canvass and by correspondence, solicited signatures to a petition to Parliament praying for relief from subscription to articles and confessions of faith, and, it is said, travelled two thousand miles in the furtherance of his object. One letter relates the progress of the scheme.

" I have received an answer to a letter I had sent to Mr. Sykes, the Vicar of Bradford, an old college acquaintance and contemporary, who writes like one fully persuaded of the righteousness of our cause, but seems restrained by doubt of its success. . . . The Master of Jesus College, Cambridge, and every resident Fellow has signed the Petition. The Bp. of Carlisle highly approved. Some members of both Houses have declared

43

their approbation of our design."   (Letter to W. Turner, sen., November 1, 1771.)

The Petition, with two hundred signatures, was presented to the House of Commons, February 6, 1772. The debate, which lasted from 2.30 P.M. to 11 P.M., was described at length in a letter to W. Turner, sen., as

" one which entered gloriously into the whole merits of our cause, and which was well worth going 240 miles to hear."

The Petition was rejected by 217 to 71. The Countess of Huntingdon had received pledges from Burke and North to oppose it. Belsham, who quotes largely from Lindsey's letter, also possessed a copy of the speeches in favour of the Petition by Sir William Meredith and Sir George Saville, written down from memory by Dr. Furneaux. The right to report Parliamentary speakers for the Press was not yet secured. Dr. Johnson, on the basis of notes taken surreptitiously, had for some years written up the speeches in the Commons for the *Gentleman's Magazine* (established 1731), and took care, as he said, " not to let the Whig dogs get the best of it." In the year before the Feathers Tavern Petition debate, several printers were arrested for publishing the debates of the House, but in 1772, after a bitter struggle, the newspapers again published reports of proceedings in Parliament, and their right has since remained unchallenged. Lindsey, in his letter, singled out Burke's speech :

" Burke declaimed most violently against us in a long speech, but entirely like a Jesuit, and full of Popish ideas ; the multifarious strange compound of the book called the Scriptures, the necessity of a priesthood, of men in society, religious as well as other, giving up their right of private judgment."

The importance of the Petition for Lindsey's future is shown in his *Apology on Resigning the Vicarage of Catterick* (1774), wherein he says : " I foresaw that if no relief was obtained, it would certainly terminate, as to myself, in the resignation of my office in the Church."

As a direct result of the debate on the Petition, two new movements for reform were set on foot—one, for the abolition of tests at the Universities, and another for the relief of Dissenters from subscription to the Articles of the Church of England as a condition of toleration. Of the first, Lindsey writes :

" As all parties in the debate agreed that the imposition upon Intrants and Graduates in our Universities was a shameful and glaring evil, our first purpose was to have this removed. Sir Wm. Meredith advised that we should leave that matter now to him and to the House, as he would bring a Bill to compel the Universities, if they would not remedy themselves. In consequence of a declaration of this sort which Sir W. M. made public, the two representatives for Cambridge University wrote to the University above a fortnight ago to advise them to take such steps as were necessary to relieve themselves. And the Chancellor, the Duke of Grafton, wrote a letter advising them to a removal of subscription to lay degrees, but to take care the established church suffered no harm." (Letter to W. Turner, sen., February 28, 1772.)

The Duke of Grafton, it may be added, eleven years after his retirement from public life, began a correspondence with Lindsey, which led to his becoming a regular attender at Essex Street Chapel.

The reform movement in the Universities made little progress. A month later, Lindsey informs Turner of the opposition it encountered :

" It is therefore apprehended that the University of Cambridge will make such delays, and conjure up such difficulties of the danger apprehended to the established church from a relaxation in the subscription for degrees, except in the case of laymen, that little or nothing will be done by them at present ; and this is the more likely, as the two Universities have entered into a friendly correspondence upon the subject, and seem determined to go hand in hand together." (April 2, 1772.)

The proceedings at Cambridge are reported a little later :

" The following extract came to me from Cambridge by the last post : ' On Sunday Mr. Thurlow's opinion came down, and the Syndicate met yesterday. He has clearly determined that the University has a right to remove subscription, and even recommends their doing it. It is presumed that he speaks, and will be looked on, as having authority, as he prudently waited the fate of the Dissenters' Bill.' " (Letter to W. Turner, sen., June 2, 1772.)

Edward Thurlow (1731–1806) was at this time Attorney-General. He became Lord Chancellor six years later.

" Since I last wrote to you, I have heard from Cambridge that the Bp. of Peterborough, the Duke of Grafton's man, who, to save the University's credit, was for a relaxation in the subscription for some degrees, is now labouring to bring the matter on again. But, as his heart is not in it out of any true Protestant principle, but pure worldly policy, and in obedience to his political masters, it is hardly expected he will succeed.

" My Tutor, Dr. Powell, now Master of St. John's College, who used to think and speak more freely, is one of the chiefs in the intrigues against any reformation. Bishop Law did vote for the removal of subscription for all degrees, whilst he stayed in the Senate, but seeing the violence with which every point was carried, went away before some of the latter graces were brought in." (Letter to W. Turner, sen., June 23, 1772.)

Lindsey and his friends were about a century before their time. Not until 1858 was it enacted that no religious test be imposed at matriculation or on taking the bachelor's degree. Candidates for M.A. and persons elected to Fellowships were still required to make the old subscription. The entire abolition of tests, after being rejected on several occasions in Parliament, was carried in 1871 by Gladstone as a Government measure.

As already stated, the failure of the Feathers Tavern Petition led to Lindsey's resignation of his living, though his doubts as to the scriptural warrant for Trinitarian worship began whilst he was at Piddle in Dorset (1756–1763). Belsham says " the first allusion which Lindsey makes to his own secret purpose of leaving the Church is in a letter dated June 2, 1772, addressed to W. Turner " :

" For my own particular, if no disposition to reform appears, and nothing be done, I do not know where things will end."

Lindsey himself, in his *Apology* (p. 210), says, " My great difficulty was the point of worship." It does not appear that the success of the Petition would have relieved Lindsey on this point. It is highly significant that when Turner, in a postscript to a letter, asked Lindsey if he had a collection of cases of persons who had refused to enter the Church on account of subscription, he replied in a letter earlier than that quoted by Belsham (April 2, 1772) that " such a collection might be of use," and suggesting the addition of the cases of those who,

than could have been expected, was over and above compensated for by the kinder construction of others. Lord North spoke out — his old argument — the disturbing things that were well — the few that were dissatisfied, only one had quitted the Church, and another, Evanson of Tewkesbury, under prosecution—the clergy of the present Church the most learned and harmonious that ever were—no Petitioners now, only a motion of Sir W. M. for they knew not who. Sir Geo. Saville replied in a most serious manner, and like a Christian, that it was not a matter of political expediency, but of high moral importance ; but his voice was so feeble, and I at a distance, that I heard imperfectly. Mr. Edmund Burke got up, made some reply to Sir George, pleaded for a strict establishment narrowly watched, but with the most unbounded toleration to Dissenters. Dwelt much on the present prosecution of Evanson, spoke highly of his moral character, but severely against him or any one else making alterations in the Liturgy, or, in the pulpit, contradicting the reading-desk. I was sorry to see this pass as the sense of the House, because it may distress some of my friends and encourage Mr. Evanson's prosecutors. Lord Geo. Cavendish got up—answered him well on the point of the necessity of a review of our Establishment, and relaxing our subscription—manly, and like a serious Christian throughout, but recurred at last to his plan on Feb. 6, 1772, of that House recommending it to the King to put the bishops on meeting the reformation that was so much wanted. Lord Caermarthen, the D. of Leeds' son, next spoke, and did very well on the court side for so young a man, pleading for an adherence to both our civil and religious establishments, with an allowance of toleration to Dissenters. Mr. Fred Montagu replied very well to him, and to some things dropped from Sir Roger Newdigate; spoke warmly and handsomely in behalf of the motion referring the matter to a Committee of Religion, which was Sir William Meredith's proposal, but declaring himself at the same time for some Articles, and speaking with high veneration of the national church. Mr. Chas. Fox adopted Burke's idea, but insisted vehemently on the Dissenters being relieved—said they had a connivance but no toleration. Sir Richd. Sutton came next, declared himself for some Articles, but an utter dislike for the present set, and gave his full vote for the motion. Sir George Germayne and others were rising, but the question was called for so loud that an end was put to the debate, and the motion rejected without a division."

Such was the end of the endeavour to reduce the terms of subscription in the established church which had its origin in the Feathers Tavern Association.

The movement to provide relief for Dissenters sprang out of a remark by Lord North in the debate of February 6, 1772, to the effect that " had a similar application been made by the Dissenting clergy, who derived no emoluments from the Church, they could see no reasonable objection to it." Dr. Philip Furneaux and Mr. Edward Pickard, who were present in the House, immediately took steps to summon the General Body of Dissenting Ministers of the three denominations, and there followed in due course a Dissenting Petition to Parliament praying for relief from subscription. W. Turner, sen., announced the early success of the movement to Lindsey, who replied (April 12, 1772) :

" I am next to thank you for transmitting to me so early intelligence of your own success in the Commons House of Parliament, which, I hope, will go through both Houses, and end in setting all Dissenting Ministers, etc., from the established church free from subscription to all articles of man's device. . . . Lord North's absenting himself, the day the motion was made, from the House, was artful and like a politic minister of State.

I do not know whether you have seen the printed Case of the Dissenters, as given to the Members on this occasion. A friend sent it to me, and remarked that Reason XII. seemed rather to be, invidiously, he said—I would say, heedlessly—given. It is this : ' Because the reasons for which Subscription is deemed necessary under an establishment do not extend to the case of a Toleration.' It seems your advocates in the House almost all have enlarged upon the difference between the two cases, yours and ours. But this could be only owing to ignorance, and political notions of religion. If they believed the Sacred Scriptures to be of divine authority, and pay any regard to the natural rights of conscience, they must relieve all subjects equally from such a yoke."

How the measure fared is related in a letter three months later (June 2, 1772), which also shows that the way of reformers is hard :

" I am much obliged by your reflections on the fate of your Bill in the Lords' House. It was a thing too much to be expected for the ruling power of this nation to establish the authority of Christ, *i.e.* of God, paramount to their own. The ignorance of some, bigotry of others, and persecuting infidelity of men will prevent anything of this kind taking place. I add these epithets to infidelity because I know some in high place, who would realize them to the utmost, if they could, upon the person of Petitioners of all sorts, and could give you proof of this, respecting myself, under black and white. You have had such encouragement from the Commons of England that it would be a shame for you to be affrighted by a Bishop's or Archbishop's staff."

The nature of the opposition, and something of the discussion, in the Upper House are given in another letter to Turner (June 23, 1773) conveying a communication received from an Episcopalian correspondent :

"Though the Dissenters have been disappointed in their first application for relief, it is by no means their intention to drop their design. . . . They were deceived by an artful administration, who acted a double part, and meant nothing less than that the Bill should pass. An approaching election rendered it necessary to conciliate the goodwill of the Dissenters. It was therefore suffered quietly to pass through the Lower House, because they knew what reception it would meet with from the Bishops. There was also a false brother of the Independent persuasion, who, spying on and envying the liberty that was arrived at, went privately with a Church of England clergyman to the Bishop of London, and gave him a false list of thirty members whom they represented as enemies to the design. This was a gross misrepresentation, for, out of 98 London ministers, there were never more than six, who, upon a division, voted against the application. It was, however, of great disservice to the cause, when mentioned in the House by the Bp. of London, who is reputed to have added to the falsehoods contained in it. . . . Your Diocesan was pleased to call the Dissenters 'a close, ambitious set of men.' Upon which Lord Chatham observed that the assertion was either true or not true. If true, his Grace ought to have produced his proofs ; if not true, he who had such sentiments of a body of men was uncharitable, and he who asserted them was a defamer. . . . I thought this extract, which seems very particular, and, I am sure, very authentic, would not be unwelcome The writer mistakes my Diocesan, who is Chester, and not his Grace the primitive Archp. of York."

When next Lindsey takes up this topic (letter to W. Turner, sen., October 6, 1774) he is himself a Dissenter, though as yet hardly realising that fact, and he speaks of the opposition to the movement of a personage even more exalted than the Archbishop of York :

"I am sorry to inform you that a negative has been put upon your application to Parliament this Session by the Committee, notwithstanding the efforts of Dr. Price, Kippis, Amory, Jefferies, etc., to the contrary. The Bp. of Carlisle told me yesterday that he heard it in great company boasted above a month ago, that the Dissenters would now be quiet, and be contented to receive at the Bishops' motion and hands hereafter what farther liberty and latitude may be thought good to allow them. . . . The King is equally stiff, and will not recede unless forced to it. . . . I heard yesterday from authority you would not doubt of, were I at liberty to name it. And, therefore, depend upon it, there will be no relief for us Dissenters this next Parliament if one man can hinder it."

The action, or rather inaction, on the part of Dissenters themselves is mentioned in a letter dated December 7, 1774:

"There was a meeting to-day of the Committee for the Dissenters at Red-Cross Library to finish what was begun last Wednesday relating to the time and manner of renewing the petition to Parliament. Dr. Calder promised to let me know what passed. From his silence, I rather conclude nothing has been determined upon." (Letter to W. Turner, sen.)

Lindsey's conclusion was correct. Whilst a third application to Parliament by the Dissenters was pending, the Roman Catholics proceeded to urge a similar claim. The tolerant attitude towards Roman Catholics which Lindsey now displayed was an advance upon his earlier opinions. In the principle of toleration, as in many matters of doctrine, he was much influenced by Priestley. On May 14, 1778, Lindsey was present in the House of Commons, and quickly reported to Turner what happened:

" I reckon the subject the House was upon was of great importance, and likely to have most useful and extensive consequences. It was a motion made by Sir George Saville and seconded by Mr. Dunning for leave to bring in a bill for relief of the Roman Catholics in respect of their worship ; to remove the penal laws against their priests for officiating, and to give them the same security for the enjoyment and disposal of their property which belongs to good subjects of a state. . . . It passed *nemine contradicente*. . . . The body of Dissenters were advised much by some of their members, who wished them well, to know whether they would take any part in the matter in putting in a petition for themselves at the same time, but they wisely resolved not to meddle at present for many reasons. And this, to my knowledge, has fixed a resolution in some of the first men in the House to take the first opportunity another Session for their effectual relief, and the full liberty of all conscientious subjects. I was much surprised to see hardly any Minister of any denomination, established or Dissenter, except myself."

Three months later, Lindsey tells Tayleur (July 28, 1778) :

" I was well informed that it was at first resolved in Council to cancel that part of the Irish Bill now depending for the relief of the Dissenters, conceding the part relating to the Roman Catholics, but they now demur, and it is thought that it will pass in the form it came."

The enactment of the measure was not forgotten during the Gordon riots of 1780, when for six days a considerable part of London was given up to pillage, and Sir George Saville's house was garrisoned by a strong body of soldiers. At the same time, it prepared the way for the success of the Dissenters' third Petition, which, as Lindsey shows, was delayed by some suspicion of Roman Catholicism :

"Two days since, I met Dr. Price at dinner at a friend's house, when I pressed him much to renew the Dissenters' application to Parliament, as I had heard from several quarters that it would be likely to succeed. He said he had heard the same : that he had talked with several of the Dissenting clergy about it, but some of them were averse to the application, as they were persuaded, if granted, it would only be with a view to give more indulgence to the Papists. I said, and he agreed, that in respect of the freedom of their worship, no one that is a Christian ought to be against it, and this should not therefore hinder them from seeking relief and security in their own case." (Letter to Tayleur, December 3, 1778.)

Next month, Lindsey again dilates on the timidity of the Dissenters :

"At one of their meetings, some of the brotherhood were coolly disposed to the matter in agitation, they made a great noise against ; said they knew not what they were about—they did not consider the ferment the late indulgence to Papists had thrown the people into—that a thing of the nature intended was not to be enterprized on the sudden, and that it would be prudent to make it known and consult the clergy about it. This you will see, Sir, was putting it off to a long day." (Letter to Tayleur, January 3, 1779.)

Finally, the bolder spirits prevailed, and within three months the Bill was in the House. In the meantime, it would appear from a letter written by Lindsey to W. Turner, sen., undated, but endorsed February 1779, that the bishops came near to taking up the case of the Dissenters :

" I have given Mr. Shore a particular account of what some of the bishops have lately nobly attempted to do for the relief of their dissenting brethren. A Bill was ready drawn, and to be brought in by the Archbishop of Canterbury for relieving dissenting ministers, etc., from the penalties of the Toleration Act, on the ground of their late petition, by subscribing their belief of the Scriptures —though some of them, far more nobly, were for no test at all. But the whole was quashed this day fortnight by your Archbishop, who spoke vehemently against it, but without any just knowledge of the subject, and was supposed to speak the sentiments of a higher personage. It is believed, however, as this opening is made, the affair will not be suffered to sleep, but taken up on the true ground—because they could not subscribe at the bidding of the civil magistrate to enjoy a right which he has no just power over them to control."

The narrative is resumed in a letter to Tayleur (March 2, 1779) :

" To-day I went down to Westminster about 3 o'clock, but was much disappointed to find no one in the Lobby of the House of Commons but the doorkeeper, from whom I learnt that the Speaker was ill, and therefore no business could be done. . . . I am rejoiced to hear that Mr. Pulteney has been addressed on the subject, and is so well disposed to it. After Bp. Ross' declaration it would be inexcusable not to pursue it with all earnestness. I hear, and am glad to hear, that they have resolved to bring it before the House, and ask it not as a favour, but a just right, and not to acquiesce in any test whatsoever."

John Ross (1719-1792), Bishop of Exeter, in a sermon before the House of Lords (January 30, 1779), had advocated an extension of toleration to Dissenters. He had also shown sympathy with the earlier attempt at a revision of the terms of subscription in the established church.

For the benefit of his Shrewsbury friend, Lindsey, who was present in the House of Commons, outlines the debate on the Bill when it next appeared there :

" Our Bill was read for the first time on Monday. Sir Roger Newdigate rose to oppose it, which he has, it seems, pledged himself to do in all its stages. But in this he is a volunteer — unprompted — which is very extraordinary, by the University of Oxford, which he represents. For Dr. Price told me the other day that he had received a letter from your worthy Dr. Adams, acquainting him that they should probably never have meddled in the business had it not been for a letter of Sir Roger's, stirring them up to it, and desiring their directions how to act. The zealous baronet repeated much of what he had urged before against the Bill, against the first reading of it, only was more violent in his criminations both of the principles and actions of the Dissenters than before. Mr. Tom Howard . . . rose up immediately after Sir Roger, and with great good sense, and in a very manly way, confuted and soon silenced him at last. He said it was the strangest proposition he had ever heard in that House, and what should not be suffered, for a member to get up and oppose the reading of a Bill which a Committee of the whole House had ordered to be brought in and read. For his part, he was quite a stranger to it. But it was on a good subject, Toleration, and he, with many others, should be glad to know what it contained. Mr. Page afterwards said a few words ex officio, I suppose, against it. And then, without anything more, it passed, and Tuesday next is the day for the second reading. It is believed it will be opposed there, and, chiefly, at the third reading, when before a Committee of the whole House, which most probably will not be till after the holidays. I am told that Lord North has intimated that he shall not be for letting it pass without annexing a test to the Scriptures : this probably to keep well with the baronets and their party, who are such sticklers against it. But you would be surprised to see how difficult it is to make the well-wishers to it understand the fitness of the large ground taken, and how any Christian can refuse to subscribe a belief of the Scriptures which he allows and preaches from. One thing will demand very serious consideration—what is to be done, if it cannot pass without a subscription such as was proposed to the former Bill. The Three Denominations of Dissenters (as I am well informed) were unanimous on the present ground, but would not be if it was narrowed. Many of them, in which number is that excellent good man Dr. Price, would, I am sure, submit to be silenced, to be imprisoned, or anything, rather than comply with a requisition from the civil magistrate to entitle him to the liberty of worshipping his Maker in his own way. . . . I forgot to tell you that Mr. Burke mentioned your humble servant by name, and, in the same breath, added that he could hardly look upon Socinians as Christians. But I must add that he did it with no ill-will, but on the contrary : and I felt not the least degree of displeasure. It came in naturally enough in reply to Sir Wm. Bagot's heat flung out against him that he had been a Papist, which he denied and proved the contrary, but added, had he changed the creed he was bred in, it would not have been to his discredit. So we were brought in civilly enough. As to his knowledge of the question—What it is to be a Christian ? You will guess, Sir, from this. ' He had been a great reader,' he said, ' a dealer in polemics—Arianism, Socinianism, etc.—but this in his younger and more rabid days, which he thought the only season for such combats, and which time he settled his mind,' which seems entirely a Christianity of E. and Athanasianism, for he reprobated the Arians also—Dr. Clarke and Whiston." (March 27, 1779.)

The fears of Lindsey as to a test being added to the Bill did not prove groundless. Three days later he reports to Tayleur :

" Our Bill has had its second reading to-day without any opposition. Its adversaries came well prepared and fortified to oppose, but agreed to let the whole rest till the next and last reading, which will be this day three weeks, when they will summon all their forces against it. Lord North desired leave to read a petition from the University of Oxford against it. Sir Philip Jennings Clarke opposed it as unfair in the Minister to bring in a thing of that kind against the reasonable demands of the Dissenters, to whom the family on the throne owed their seat, when the Papists were indulged so lately in their liberty without any opposition. It was, however, read. I could not distinctly hear it. But the purport was to express their concern for the education of youth especially being, by the Bill depending, to be put into the hands of men, who did not so much as give assurance to the public that they believed the Scriptures : praying against suffering a Bill to pass which gave teachers of youth and preachers of religion such unlimited degree of liberty. Lord North added that it passed in a very full Convocation without any opposition. As this last named Lord is thus enlisted against the Bill, and expected to exert himself on that side, the friends to it should be exhorted to be firm and strenuous on their part."

A letter to Samuel Shore, of Norton, near Sheffield, one of the original Trustees of Essex Street Chapel, gives a good report of the third reading :

" Yesterday was a day of good debate. Lord North opened with the proposal of a test, that the Minister, etc., should acknowledge himself a Christian and a Protestant, and declare that the Holy Scriptures, commonly received by Protestant Churches, contained a revelation of the whole

will of God, and that he would take them for the rule
of his doctrine and practice.   For the Bill as it was without a Test, Sir Henry Houghton, Mr. Wilkes, Mr.
Dunning, Mr. Charles Fox, Mr. Sergt. Adair, Mr.
Charles Turner, Lord John Cavendish, Sir Wm. Meredith, Mr. Goodriche were the speakers.   Sir Henry
Houghton endeavoured to show that the imposition of
such a Test was without the magistrate's province.   Mr.
Wilkes was well heard in his defence of the most unlimited toleration, which he enlivened with many pleasant
and witty remarks on Athanasius and the Thirty-Nine
Articles.   Mr. Dunning was full of excellent, close
reasoning, but more feeble in his voice, and not so
animated and pointed as I have heard him.   Mr. Fox
excelled all men but himself in depth, force, and clearness
of argument, and demonstrated the utter wrongness of
the civil magistrate requiring any Test whatsoever as a
condition of enjoying so natural and inalienable a right
as that of worshipping God according to a man's own
conscience.   The rest spoke very well.   On the other
side, after Lord North were a Mr. Croyts, member for
the University of Cambridge, who said a few words ;
Mr. Powys, member for Northamptonshire ; Mr. Burke,
Sir Adam Ferguson, the Lord-Advocate for Scotland.
Mr. Burke spoke admirably well, kept close to his point
and with fewer digressions than I ever knew him, made
use of a great deal of plausible reasoning, not without
some artifice, to whom the unaccountable peevishness
and perverseness of men's refusing to subscribe what they
did believe—never alluding to the just objection some
minds might make to do it at the bidding of the civil
magistrate.   He also dwelt long, and with more reason,
on the inconsistency of objecting to subscribe the Scriptures at the command of the magistrate, and yet making
no objection to the Declaration against Papacy, but he
dwelt upon it as an Orator, to make the most of it, not
considering that it is generally looked upon in a civil
light.   However, as it was, I am persuaded that this

gentleman gave a turn to the House, and the Test is to be ascribed to him, not that I think he did not speak his own sentiments sincerely, but, with all his knowledge and parts, he presumes he knows more than he does. The numbers were : For the Test, 88 ; against it, 58. When the matter is to be brought in again, I have not heard, nor what further steps are to be taken. The Cavendishes all stayed and divided against the Test. Sir Geo. Saville was not returned to Town from his regiment."

In a letter written eight days later to Tayleur, Lindsey covers much the same ground, with the following addition :

" One thing I was glad to hear Lord North advance, which it was that it had been apprehended without that this Bill would put those worthy persons that could not come up to it in a worse condition than they were before, but he could venture to tell them that they had nothing to fear from those in power, and that the temper of the times would still be their security."

The last observation helps to explain the unchallenged freedom of men like Lindsey and Priestley in preaching Unitarianism whilst it was still an offence against the law to do so. The declaration required by the new Toleration Act of 1797 was somewhat ambiguous. " What liberal Dissenters had in their breasts peeps out when they argue that the Scriptures ' contain ' the revealed will of God, embedded in some other matter, and that they receive ' the same,' *videlicet*, the will of God (not the Scriptures at large) as their rule." [1] Lindsey, for his part, as his letters prove, was against the Test, such as it was, which the Act imposed upon the Dissenters.

[1] Gordon, *Heresy : Its Ancient Wrongs and Modern Rights*, p. 73.

The interest which Lindsey displayed in schemes of ecclesiastical reform in Ireland, and his views on church establishment in that country, are exhibited in a letter to Tayleur (September 1, 1783) :

" I have lately had a letter from Scotland, which says that at their meeting this present month at Dungannon, their Irish neighbours propose to attempt some reformation in matters ecclesiastical as well as civil : that their Delegates are to have under consideration a scheme for dividing the tithes of that kingdom into three parts—one to the present established church, one for Protestant Dissenters, a third for Roman Catholics—the plan to take effect as the present Incumbents drop off. The Bp. of Derry (Lord Bristol) is chosen delegate for Londonderry, and will support the plan with all his might. Another part of the same scheme is to allow Patrons to present persons of all denominations to Church livings, requiring no other obligation than to acknowledge the divine authority of the Old and New Testaments. Whether this takes place or no immediately, it shows the dispositions of unprejudiced men, and may open a way to shake the hierarchy, which, by its vast revenues is, and would be for ever, the support of religious tyranny. I do not wonder that it strikes the Irish as monstrous that the clergy of the establishment should have all the tithes, when nine-tenths of the people at least are of a different religious persuasion."

It does not appear that the plan outlined by Lindsey ever entered the domain of practical politics. He attributes it, in a letter to Tayleur a month later, to the Irish volunteers. In the second application of Dissenters to Parliament for the repeal of the Corporation and Test Acts of 1661 and 1673, which excluded Nonconformists from office in any municipal body and from all employment under the Government, Lindsey, Priestley, and other Unitarians took a prominent part. The first application for repeal, made more than half a century before (March 12, 1738) had been defeated by 251 to 123 in the Commons. From 1727 onwards, annual Indemnity Acts were passed in favour of those who had failed to qualify themselves under the Corporation and Test Acts. Writing to Tayleur (March 2, 1787) six days before Beaufoy introduced the second application in the House, Lindsey thus discusses its prospects :

"What is of more consequence is the intended Bill this day week to be brought in for the repeal of the Corporation and Test Acts, and the providing such support for it as may secure it from contempt. I will tell you, Sir, what I have been informed of, from good authority relating to it, within the course of this week. The King is said to be most vehemently against it, which was rather expected, as he is said not to love the Dissenters. Mr. Pitt was at first rather inclined, but is now averse to it. Bp. Prettyman, I am well assured, one day read over with him the republication of Sherlock's in favour of the Corporation and Test Acts, an artful piece, and his arguments are said to have swayed entirely not only with the Minister, but all his young friends, as they are called—Mr. Barker, Elliott, etc., who will all be against the Bill. There is no mention of their having looked into Hoadley's answer to it. There is, however, an abridgment of Hoadley drawing up by an able hand, which will be printed and sold on Saturday, but not before, which I am sorry for, and will be sent to each member of Parliament. . . . You would observe in the papers Dr. Horsley's intended publication against the Dissenters' case, which they have circulated. It is unquestionably true that this, and his merits to the Church of England, have procured him his Prebend, and will further advance him. Bp. Hurd, to whom the king listens much, says that the Dissenters are under no persecution, that they have no reason to complain of the Church ; that they would be well advised in being quiet and doing nothing to create enmity in the Church against them. This I had from one to whom the Bp. said this and more. Lord Beauchamp at first promised strenuous assistance. They had reckoned upon him to have seconded Mr. Beaufoy, but yesterday they found not only that he declined it, but also that his lordship was going into the country, and should take no part in the question. I am sorry to mention that many old Whigs of my acquaintance in the House, through resentment, I think, at the Dissenters having conspired to bring in Mr. Pitt and his party, have resolved either to absent themselves or to vote against the Bill. I must except Lord George Cavendish. Some of them pretend fear of riot, and of the return of the confusions of the year 1789. . . . Our Committee of gentlemen were to apply to Mr. Pulteney to second Mr. Beaufoy. It is given out that the Bill will not be permitted to have a second reading or go to a Committee, but will be thrown out instantly. The bigotry and ignorance relating to this plain question which one hears of and meets is astonishing."

Sir Henry Houghton seconded the motion moved by Beaufoy. Fox supported it. North and Pitt spoke in opposition, and the motion was rejected by 178 to 100. Priestley, who heard the debate, addressed a letter to Pitt on some of the sentiments expressed by him. A third application (May 8, 1789) was again negatived, the votes being 122 to 102. Fox made the fourth application (March 2, 1790), which was rejected by 294 to 105. It was on this occasion that he arrived, booted and whip in hand, from Newmarket, and made what was probably his most eloquent speech in the House of Commons.

In 1791 the Roman Catholics secured another measure of relief. The attitude of Dissenters towards the Bill is seen from the following letter :

F

" On Friday last, the Deputies of the Dissenters in England and Wales, resident in London, held a meeting, in which they came to a resolution to address the Catholics now petitioning Parliament, that although they themselves had been disappointed, they most cordially wished them success in their present application, and should truly rejoice in their obtaining. This resolution was communicated to the Catholics by their Chairman, and produced an answer, which I saw to-day, from their body assembled, thanking the Dissenters for their kindness to them, and for their very seasonable encouragement ; implying as if they had rather expected opposition from that quarter. . . . It is expected that there will be a good debate in the House upon the subject to-day. Some say that the Minister will try to put a stop to the business, foreseeing that it will involve him in difficulties respecting the Dissenters. We shall soon see, however, what he does. And do what he will, truth will get the better of him." (Letter to Tayleur, March 1, 1791.)

The Chairman of Deputies at this meeting was Michael Dodson, one of the first members of Essex Street Chapel, and appointed a Trustee thereof in December 1792. A curious proviso in the Bill, referring to Unitarians, is mentioned in Lindsey's next despatch to Shrewsbury :

" You may perhaps have seen the printed Heads of the Bill now pending in the Commons House for the Relief of Protesting Catholic Dissenters. Among the conditions and restrictions near the close of it is the following Proviso : ' That the Act shall not extend to persons writing against the Trinity.' Now what have Catholics to do with such a clause ? They are known Trinitarians. They cannot be otherwise. The truth is, this article did not come from the Catholics themselves, but was imposed upon them. This they told a Member of Parliament upon his questioning them concerning this. It was thought, however, that such a strange thing, which had caused surprise in some, might have been dropped when the Bill was first read on Thursday last. But the same Member of Parliament took particular notice its being repeated by the Speaker in reading it. It will certainly not be forgotten at the second reading in the House of Commons, nor, I can add, when it comes to the Upper House. But what low cunning this—to lug in, by a side wind, a second confirmation at a hundred years' distance by Parliament of an Act so shocking that the time will not suffer the most forward orthodoxy to put in execution, merely to hang it up *in terrorem* against those who write against the Trinity." (Letter to Tayleur, March 12, 1791.)

"The restriction about the Trinity, which I mentioned as foisted into the Bill for the relief of the Catholics, is said to have been put in by the Chancellor, to make their toleration correspond with that of the Protestant Dissenters : but I hope no such excuse will pass. I have been told that Lord Stanhope intends to notice it in the Upper House. I had before been told that another Lord would speak his mind upon it. I wish the former would consult with and act in concert with his brethren, else he may do harm, where he intends good, and prevent or defeat the exertions of others in the cause."

A little later Lindsey writes :

"How much to be esteemed is Mr. Fox ? Upon the Catholic Dissenters Bill last night, among other excellent things, he declared his intention of bringing in a Bill on better and more extensive principles for the relief of Protestant as well as Catholic Dissenters if the Ministry would not undertake it." (Letter to Tayleur, April 7, 1791.)

It was not, however, until 1828, upon the fifth application of Dissenters for relief, that the repeal of the Corporation and Test Acts was carried, on the motion of Lord John Russell, and became law on May 9 in that year.

The efforts of the Scottish Presbyterians at this time to secure freedom from Tests was brought to the notice of Lindsey by his correspondents in Scotland, and duly reported to Tayleur :

" The other day I met Dr. Somerville, one of the ministers from Scotland to carry on their application to Parliament for relief from the Test Laws.   He does not think they shall succeed, but expects their cause will be well argued and supported.   One thing, however, I was glad to hear, because the contrary had been reported, that they will not secede from their purpose, nor accept of any other religious test, in lieu of the present, nor of any religious test at all."   (May 7, 1791.)

A fortnight later he speaks of

" the very rude treatment which the Scotch Deputies met with from the Minister and House of Commons in their rejection of their Petition. . . ."

Then follows a transcription of part of a letter from a Scottish correspondent describing the discussion of the Petition in the General Assembly :

" The matter of the Test Act was compromised between the heads of the two parties.   The Ministerial party intended a vote of censure on the Committee, who had applied to Parliament, for not presenting the Petition according to their instruction.   They were to choose the earliest and the properest time.   And that could never, they maintained, be the properest time, when they knew previously they should meet with a refusal, and which they knew to be offensive to government.   The popular party, on the other hand, intended to move a vote of thanks to the Committee for their proper conduct. The heads met together previously the night before, and had very high debates.   They were mutually, the

Moderator tells me, afraid of each other. The Ministerial party not without fear of a defeat, but still more of
a discussion, when the minds of men were so agitated.
For it is now, the Moderator thinks, in the power of the
popular leaders, by the least exertion, to raise a tumult
equal to any in Charles the First's days. The popular
party were not without fear of a defeat if it came to a
vote ; they agreed, therefore, if the Ministerial party
would withdraw their vote of censure, they would that
of thanks. Only one person, a lawyer, spoke. He said
it was the most extraordinary occurrence in the annals
of history for government to refuse the prayers of a whole
nation. But he was always averse to their being presented, from a conviction that it was needless, he being
of opinion—and he was supported by the best authorities
in the kingdom—that the Test Laws have no operation
on Scottish men, members of the Kirk establishment.
The moment he had done, a creature of Dundas moved
the next question. The popular party think they have
gained a triumph, the question being still open, and will
most assuredly come on the next Assembly. The
Ministerial party endeavour to soothe them by douceurs.
They have given the Clergy an exemption from the late
house tax, and are promising them an augmentation of
stipend. But this will not quiet the lay-members, nor
the ruffled minds of the kingdom. And you may be
assured that the Test Act must very shortly, within a
year or two, be repealed, if it be not already virtually
so by nullity of effect on Presbyterians. A trial in the
King's bench would bring this to a decision at once."

The last reform movement with which Lindsey was
associated was that for legalising Unitarianism. Early
in 1791 was formed the Unitarian Society for promoting
Christian Knowledge, of which Lindsey and his friends
were the leading spirits and Tayleur a generous patron.
Steps were quickly taken to secure, if possible, the repeal

of the laws against Unitarians. The inception, progress, and result of the movement may be traced in Lindsey's letters :

"To-morrow there is to be a general meeting of the members of our Unitarian Society to consider of a Petition to Parliament for the repeal of the laws against Antitrinitarians. Mr. Dodson, Dr. Priestley, and another person were last Thursday appointed to draw up a Petition to be offered to the meeting, and the former of these has drawn up a very proper one. Whether it is to be presented or no this Session is undetermined. Mr. Fox has very obligingly offered his services (which, however, we do not mention but to friends), and advised this mode of application. There is a printed paper which Dr. Priestley had seen from some High Churchmen inviting all that wish well to the establishment to unite against the efforts that are making against it by Socinians, Republicans, Deists, etc." (Letter to Tayleur, February 15, 1792.)

Twelve days later, Lindsey writes to the same correspondent :

"Our friend undertook to send you the Petition, otherwise I should have done it. . . . I am glad you are exerting yourself to procure a good number of signatures at Shrewsbury. . . . To-day, in the street, I met Dr. Kippis ; he told me he had not seen the Petition, whereas I should have hoped it would have been laid in the Vestry at his Meeting to be signed yesterday, as it was at ours. We had about thirty names, and I should hope shall have about thirty or forty more."

On March 26, 1792, Lindsey writes :

"It is still thought by not a few that our Petition to the Commons will succeed. Dr. Heberden told me the other day that he had been pressing, upon the subject, a member of some note, bred at Oxford, proving to him that instead of hurting, such a step would be a security to the Church, and his friend replied to him that he had not heard anything against it, and that he believed, if Mr. Pitt did not directly oppose, it would pass. I was much pleased the other day with a sight of your two grandsons to the copy of the Petition. . . . I have received 400 names from different quarters to be added to the 1600 with which Mr. Fox first announced it. We do not find any day yet fixed for bringing the business on, and, it is imagined, it will not be till the return of the lawyers from the circuit."

Addressing W. Turner, jun., May 4, 1792, Lindsey says :

" I assured myself, without all question, that I should have been able with this cover to convey to you an account of the fate of our present application to Parliament ; which you, who have taken so much pains to support with names, had some claims to be acquainted with, but Mr. Pitt, by putting the affair off till this day, has defeated my purpose. Rumour will have it that the Minister postponed it to consult the Cabinet and the Bishops, and with a view to let our Petition be granted, as a sop to Cerberus, to quiet all grumblings. . . . Others say the Bishops and a Great Personage will never consent to such a slur being put upon the doctrine of the Trinity as to take off all penalties for writing and speaking against it. We shall see, however, what comes to pass."

The following day, Lindsey writes to Shrewsbury on the same topic :

" I have seen no paper, nor any person, to give an account how our Petition fared in the House under our noble leader, who presented and patronized it. But it was believed the Minister would accede to the repeal of the more obnoxious statutes to pacify the murmurs which his Monday's speech and declaration against all reform of Parliament has excited. . . . I find from the morning paper that Mr. Fox put off the bringing in of our Petition till the next Friday, being too much indisposed to attend the House. I hope the vast number that have twice wasted many hours to secure a place will not be wearied out."

Fox's motion (May 11, 1792) was defeated by 142 to 63. Burke spoke strongly against it, describing Unitarians as allies of the Jacobins and disciples of Tom Paine. He declared that they " are associated for the express purpose of proselytism," aiming " to collect a multitude sufficient by force and violence to overturn the Church," and this " concurrent with a design to subvert the State." He begged the House not to wait " till the conspirators, met to commemorate the 14th July, shall seize on the Tower of London and the magazines it contains, murder the governor and the mayor of London, seize upon the King's person, drive out the House of Lords, occupy your gallery, and thence, as from an high tribunal, dictate to you."

A letter to Tayleur briefly narrates what followed the failure of the Petition :

" We met together on a public call to consider what steps were to be taken in consequence of our late Petition to Parliament. . . . The result of the meeting was a series of resolutions returning thanks to Mr. Fox principally, and to the other gentlemen who so nobly supported our cause, and to signify to our brethren and friends that we should by no means give up, but pursue it at the next Session, though nothing was determined particularly in what mode this was to be done, but another meeting appointed on that day fortnight to settle it."

Lindsey did not live to see the success of this effort. It was not until twenty-one years later that the profession of Unitarianism was legalised. The Bill, introduced into the House by William Smith, the grandfather of Florence Nightingale, received the royal assent on July 21, 1813.

CHAPTER IV

LINDSEY AND POLITICS

IT is a matter of considerable interest and of some historical importance to note in Lindsey's letters his many allusions to two of the greatest events in modern history : the revolutions in America and in France. His attitude towards both may be stated in a single sentence. He was the intimate friend of Joseph Priestley and Richard Price, and a frequent associate of Benjamin Franklin.

Writing June 13, 1774, he informs W. Turner, sen., that he had dined on the previous Friday with Dr. Price.

" He is quite dispirited, as all serious, good citizens are, with the closing transactions of this Session, especially the Canada Bill. And we have now nothing but intestine troubles and the miseries of a sinking, profligate, impoverished State to look to."

The Canada Bill, otherwise the Quebec Act, was the work of Lord North. It satisfied the aspirations of the French colonists, preserving their traditional customs, religion, and institutions, but at the expense of the territorial ambitions of the older colonies, and involving the denial to English settlers of the rights of self government to which they laid claim.

A few months later, Lindsey's sympathy with the Americans is stated most clearly :

" This sudden dissolution of Parliament is reckoned an artful political manœuvre, and the more so, as the secret has been so well kept that I do not find that any one in this wide city, nor I suppose, out of it, had the least suspicion of it till Thursday night, after the Council had broken up, that it was revealed to a few that a new Parliament was to be called instantly. The most probable motives assigned for it are the apprehension of a general ferment through the nation, and requisition from their representatives of the like stipulation which Wilkes and Glynn have made, especially with regard to American measures which our infuriated Ministry is said still to persist in their resolution not to retract, and, as I hope and believe, the Americans will not yield and submit, I trust their oppressors will be routed and confounded. Dr. Price told me a few days ago that he had that day seen a Coventry merchant, who assured him that if the breach with America went on widening, and they would not take our goods, he must soon turn off a hundred hands upon the public. This is only one instance of the certain fatal consequence of our intended firmness. It is believed the Ministry will carry no point in the city of London, nor in Middlesex, though it is lamented the friends of liberty are divided." (Letter to W. Turner, sen., October 6, 1774.)

Lindsey's conjecture as to the reason for the sudden dissolution of Parliament, September 30, proved to be correct. The King wanted a new Parliament elected before any doubt should arise in the mind of the public as to the success of his American policy, and his scheme proved successful. Wilkes and Glynn were, however, returned unopposed for Middlesex.

On November 3, 1774, Lindsey speaks of Franklin, who had been present at the first service held in Essex Street Chapel on the previous April 17.

" I have called three times lately on Dr. Franklin, but unlucky in missing him. Dr. Price had seen him the day before, when he told him that they were going on at the Congress with cool ardour and firmness. Many thanks for your intelligence from Boston, which is highly agreeable to me for the good testimony to the much injured Americans, and also to my quondam pupil, Lord Percy. I must not forget to tell you that I heard it attested by a person of character in a public company the other day that Governor Hutchinson, the enemy of the Bostonians, able, but most artful, is often closeted by a Certain Person, and has been rewarded with a pension of £200 a year."

A fortnight later, Lindsey and Priestley dined with Mr. Timothy Hollis, when Mr. Brand Hollis read

" part of two letters he had received before from a Tutor of the University, and from Dr. Chauncey, Minister of the First Church in Boston. They were both very affecting—full of deepest apprehension for themselves and their own, and for the parent country. They complained of having been misrepresented as seeking to be independent. They never wished it, but gloried in the contrary, but that for ten years past there had been a series of measures to oppress and irritate, and that these last Acts had completed the schemes of despotism and slavery they had been so long threatened with. But that it would never do. Nine-tenths of that province and of the rest of the colonies were firm against it on enlightened principles ; that the people in the colony were hardly restrained from flying out into acts of desperation on seeing a standing army sent amongst them, and their port locked up, and they looked upon this as a sample of the government intended for them—that they feared England would not reverse her acts and measures in time to prevent the worst, and when the sword was once drawn, farewell to all cordiality or their regard for their oppressors." (Letter to W. Turner, sen., November 17, 1774.)

Timothy Hollis, F.R.S., was the youngest son of John Hollis, the third son of Thomas Hollis, the founder of the Hollis family. He was an intimate friend of Lindsey, who informed Tayleur on one occasion that " Mr. Timothy Hollis, our near neighbour, a most friendly and worthy person, has given me a general invitation every day and for any part of it." His uncle, the second Thomas, was a most generous benefactor of Harvard College, Cambridge, Massachusetts. Having no direct heir, he bequeathed his property to his nephew Thomas, the son of Nathaniel, the second son of the founder of the family, who became the father of Thomas Hollis (1720–1774), " Republican," who lavished his means on books and portraits, which he presented to various colleges. Amongst his gifts was the portrait of Sir Isaac Newton to Trinity College, Cambridge, and the famous portrait of Cromwell to Sidney Sussex College, Cambridge. In theology he was a liberal, and a friend and correspondent of Lindsey, whose father-in-law, Archdeacon Blackburne, was his biographer. He bequeathed his wealth to his friend Thomas Brand, who assumed the name of Hollis, the recipient of the letters from which Lindsey quotes. At his death, he willed his estates, worth £5000 a year, to John Disney, Lindsey's brother-in-law and colleague at Essex Street Chapel.

Charles Chauncey, D.D. (1705–1787), one of the writers of the letters in question, was the great-grandson of the second President of Harvard College, an ardent supporter of the patriots during the War of Independence, and a precursor of New England Unitarianism.

The opening of the conflict with America is quickly related :

" The report of the day is that the Packet that is arrived has brought an account of an engagement at Boston, in which we have been worsted. In consequence of this, it is said three battalions of the Guards are to be immediately sent over under General Amherst, who is to supersede Gage. Farewell to old England's greatness if the sword is drawn and blood shed in America. What will three battalions, or thirty battalions do ? But our infatuation is astonishing. There is not the least symptom of kindness or humanity towards our brethren in America from the throne, or in the speeches of Ministerial people, but all war and vengeance. Mr. B. Hollis, who called just now and gave me this frank, says that the cause of the Americans was nobly supported in the House by Col. Barre, who laid open the whole of the Ministerial conduct towards America, and exposed their pretended contempt of the Americans as soldiers, which he could well do, as having served amongst them. But all reason and eloquence is in vain against a bribed majority. Nothing but calamity seems capable to awaken us out of our unfeelingness towards justice and our true interests. And that seems to be coming." (Letter to W. Turner, sen., December 7, 1774.)

Gage was superseded by Sir William Howe, who landed on Charlestown peninsula, June 17, 1775. Parliament opened on November 30, and Lindsey relates in his letter that he

" was at Westminster Hall on Monday to have heard the debate, but a Scotch Baronet moved to have the House cleared, and, though many of the members opposed it, he would not recede, and above a hundred of us were dismissed."

The support which the oppressive measures of the English Government received in the country is plain from Lindsey's admissions :

" I am grieved, and so also is Dr. Price, at your account
of the temper of almost all about you (at Wakefield)
towards the much injured and persecuted Americans.
They will, however, vindicate their own cause, and we
shall see the justice of it when poverty and our own
interest has opened our eyes.   I dined yesterday in company with Drs. Price, Priestley, Franklin, and Mr. Quincy.
We began and ended with the Americans.   Mr. Q.
was large on the subject.   He read four or five long
letters lately received from persons of worth and eminence
in New England—all of which concurred to assure us
that our brethren on the other side of the Atlantic *will
be free*.   There were several particulars, not safe for this
conveyance, which will confirm not only the bravery but
the wisdom of the heads of that colony at the present
critical moment.   The Ministry are said to be still resolved to persevere, and to change nothing till some news
from America puts them upon it ; and, what is perhaps
not extraordinary considering the influence of the Crown,
they seem to hold themselves to be immortal."   (Letter
to W. Turner, sen., January 17, 1775.)

Josiah Quincy (1744–1775), American patriot, who
was one of the dinner party mentioned by Lindsey, took
a prominent part, as journalist and popular leader, in the
proceedings at Boston that heralded the outbreak of war.
After the " Boston Massacre " (March 3, 1770), he and
John Adams defended Captain Preston and the accused
soldiers, who fired on the mob, and secured their acquittal.
In September 1774 he left for England in order to consult with leading Whigs as to the political situation in
America.   On March 16, 1775, he started back, but
died April 26, in sight of land.

We now hear of the famous speech of Chatham on
the American question, and some interesting particulars
of affairs in Massachusetts :

" You will have read an account of Lord Chatham's
noble motion and incomparable speech upon it, well
seconded by Lords Shelburne, Camden, Richmond,
Rockingham, etc. But all is to no purpose. Vengeance
is decreed against the Americans if they will not submit.
Three regiments—one of light horse—six hundred
mariners—six sloops of war to course along the coast,
are immediately to be sent. Providence seems to permit
our present Ministry to hasten our ruin and the independence of America. And, it may be, if so, certainly will
be, for the best. And we may all of us have reason to
rejoice that there will be a place in the globe where
Englishmen may be free. I have seen a gentleman to-
day, who gave an authentic account of a letter from an
officer in the army at Boston, which represented their
situation extremely disagreeable and even unsafe, on
account of the increased resentment of the whole country
at their continuance amongst them—that they were
extremely careful to give no offence designedly, though
they could not sometimes avoid doing it—that, though
they had no great numbers of desertions hitherto, they
apprehended they should soon have many, as the Bostonians
were very assiduous to entice them, not by empty promises,
but by assurances of good support—of land to settle upon
and of each a wife also, to settle upon it." (Letter to
W. Turner, sen., January 26, 1775.)

When writing of the freedom which an independent
America might provide for Englishmen, Lindsey little
thought before twenty years had passed his dearest friend,
in his own words, " seeing no prospect of doing much
good or having much enjoyment in this country," should
be driven to find a refuge in America.

On February 20, Lord North moved a resolution to
the effect that if any colony provided what Parliament
considered its fair proportion towards the common defence
and the expenses of its civil administration, no duty or

tax should be imposed upon it, except for the regulation of trade. It was an attempt to meet the colonists half-way. Lindsey shared the view of it expressed by Burke and other opponents in the House, as his letter written eight days later indicates :

" The measures of our infatuated administration are carrying into execution. One sees the red-coats preparing themselves in Hyde Park and St. James' every day. Their rulers are persuaded that the Americans, the Bostonians in particular, will throw down their arms at the sight of our troops. My acquaintance, who are better informed, say quite the reverse. This is, however, the expectation of the government. They reckon also much upon the Associations of the friends of the government in America. But my acquaintance say these will be as airy as their other reckonings. Lord North's motion is reckoned ill-judged, as well as base and insidious—ill-judged, because the Americans will not be deceived by it—and it is a vile resource to sow discord and dissension amongst fellow-subjects, in order to carry their measures, which, if just, would be better secured by fair and just expedients. A friend told me that Lord North worded the motion so as to leave them to infer that it was that of One Personage, and that he had it immediately from him." (Letter to W. Turner, sen., February 28, 1775.)

After a break in the extant letters to Turner, Lindsey thus refers to the American Revolution :

" There is nothing new relating to America which has transpired, though it is believed that late accounts have been received by the Government. We shall see if to-night's ' Gazette ' reveal anything. It is a general opinion that the Americans are so strong that they will keep their ground at New York, and baffle your attempts at Philadelphia, and that General Burgoyne will not pass the Lakes, and come on the back settlements so speedily

habitants in a week had come to the parish, having no work to be employed in. It is still worse at Kidder-minster—one thousand have migrated elsewhere, and in the streets where you used to meet crowds you now meet as we make him. Yet, nevertheless, we are pursuing the war here with redoubled vengeance, and, it is said, have taken more foreign troops in pay. What infatuation! Calamity has already invaded some families I know, and will invade many more e'er long, and what will be the end of such measures is too easy to foretell,

only a passenger or two. How it is in the North you can tell. Many very respectable persons, merchants, my friends, are constrained, some to leave Town and retire into the country, others to quit their country houses. Few but contractors and their appertainers flourish, and they continue to vilify the Americans, and cry out for the war."

The position at this time seemed quite desperate to friends of America and lovers of peace.

"Sir Geo. Saville is not come to attend his seat in Parliament, quite despairing of any benefit of opposition in the prostrate state of affairs in our country, and the determined obstinacy by a venal majority to carry on the cruel, arbitrary measures of the court, not more unchristian than impolitic, as happily they have hitherto missed their aim in enslaving America, of which their design the Quebec Act was no obscure prelude." (Letter to Tayleur, December 3, 1778.)

On July 23, 1779, we hear the first whisper of negotiations for peace.

"Concerning our public affairs, there seems now nothing to be done but to wait the long foretold effects of our mad and wicked measures. One aggravation of them I heard this very morning from a friend, who had just been with one in high place, who informed him, with regret, that a few months ago, through the mediation of Spain for a peace, who were sincere in it, you had such honourable terms offered from the Americans by Dr. Franklin as were really as much as you ought to have, and more than you could expect. The first preliminary was a suspension of arms for ten years. But it was to be understood you were not to be immediately required to acknowledge the independence of America, nor were you required to withdraw your troops, but at your own leisure and as you pleased—in short, these two grand articles were to be settled by negociation. And a general amnesty

was to be passed, which would have secured those who
had declared for you. And they were under no such
restrictions to trade as to hinder your coming into what
would be as much as you ought to have thought—not all
you possessed before. The ministry, many of them were
for it, but not One Man, and so it dropped, and a more
extensive, bloody war is commenced, the end of which
no one knows who shall live to see. I do not find that
there is any news in Town from America, the West
Indies, or Admiral Hardy ; more than you have had for
some time in the public prints. We were in a little
panic here when Spain first declared against you that we
were going to be invaded. But that and all other fears
and even murmurs are gone, and people in general are
satisfied with the proceedings of the Government here,
as they seem to be in the country, which undoubtedly
has been, and is, an encouragement for them to go on in
the ruinous war they have begun. The friend who told
me the above, says that Lord Mountstuart is certainly
intended to go to Petersburgh, but he (my friend) had no
doubt but the French, in their late mediation of Peace
betwixt Russia and the Porte, took care to tie the hands
of the former with respect to interfering in their quarrel
with England." (Letter to Tayleur.)

The surrender of Cornwallis at Yorktown, October 19,
1781, virtually ended the war. Rockingham formed his
Cabinet, with Fox as Secretary for Foreign Affairs, on
March 24. Six days afterwards, Lindsey gives his friend
some assurance of the coming peace :

"Some pretty high in the administration are of my old
Cambridge acquaintance. Their firm purpose—to put
an end to this wanton, bloody war—gives one pleasure."
(Letter to Tayleur.)

Three days later (April 2, 1782) he writes in more
detail to his clerical brother at Wakefield :

" I am persuaded that you will have no less pleasure
than we all here in the late changes in the Ministry. We
are told that the new officers of State are indefatigable.
Mr. Fox has given up all his gaming connections, and is
in his office by seven in the morning.   Peace, if possible,
they will aim at.   But, in order to secure it, they must
prepare for war.   Dr. Price this day told me that he saw
a letter yesterday from Amsterdam with great satisfaction,
and plainly intimated a hope that it would bring about a
speedy reconciliation between the two nations.   This will
be a fortunate event, as the Dutch are known to be
formidable, and are much to be dreaded, that some
disaster will befall us from them sometime in this month,
if some pacifying message be not sent to them. . . . Mr.
Lee was sent for by express from the Lancaster Assizes,
and arrived in Town on Saturday night.   But no appointment has yet taken place with regard to the places of
Attorney and Solicitor-General, one of which he is
supposed to be designed for, if he choose it."

Preliminary articles of peace between Great Britain
and the colonies were signed November 30, 1782.
Lindsey's letters on the war with America reveal his
warm sympathy with the colonies, his strong abhorrence
of the policy of King George and Lord North, and the
general excellence of the information respecting persons
and events which he imparted to his correspondents.   A
year later, he shows himself to be again in touch with
representative Americans

" After breakfast to-day, I walked towards Dr. Jebb's,
Parliament Street, and had the good luck to meet the
famous Mr. Adams, Minister for the United States at
the Hague, with one or two other Americans I knew.
He is a grave but agreeable character, not talkative, but
not shy or dark, and, I believe, will endeavour that the
interests of England and America may be united, and

that their excellent plans for their American government may be established and improved. . . . It was not Mr. Adams who spoke at the Revolution Club on Tuesday, but an American, Mr. Gorham, whom Dr. Price had introduced."

John Adams (1735–1826) was appointed to The Hague in July 1780, and there secured recognition of the United States as an independent Government (April 19, 1782). In 1785 he was appointed the first Minister to the Court of St. James. Eleven years later, he was elected second President of the United States.

Gorham took a leading part, as a representative of Massachusetts, in the Convention which settled the constitution of the United States (1776–1789).

A pleasant reminiscence of the war with America appears in a letter sent to Tayleur February 10, 1784, wherein he speaks of a friend :

" Mr. Wren, Dissenting Minister at Portsmouth, within a few months made Dr., from the College of New Jersey in America, which was transmitted to him with a letter from the President of the Congress, thanking him in their name and that of all America for his humane attention to their prisoners in hold in England. There is no doubt but that he was instrumental in saving the lives of many hundreds as well as relieving thousands. His friends are jocose with him, and he has been much pleased with several letters from persons who had returned to different parts in America, acquainting him that Providence had blessed them with sons, and that they had taken the liberty to christen them Thomas Wren. He is a Unitarian, inclined to the Arian side, but rather veering, and in vast esteem with all that know him, his wit being as sound as his excellent religious principles."

Thomas Wren, D.D., was minister of Portsmouth (High Street Chapel) from 1757 to 1787.

The general sympathy of Lindsey and his circle with the French Revolution in its early stages is indicated in a letter dated May 21, 1791, nearly two years after Louis XVI. had opened the meeting of the States General.

" It is not easy to describe the panic fears that are entertained by many at the West end of the Town of Dissenters—Unitarians—favourers of the French Revolution, as if the like war to be brought about in the same way, and that particularly the meeting to celebrate the anniversary of the French Revolution, the 14th of August, is the time assigned for the commencement of it, and a confederation at home.   Those who invent these things, I suppose, serve their own purposes, but they often contribute to raise the ferment they would pretend to allay. I am glad, however, that the conductors of this annual celebration will not be wanting to use every precaution against disturbances of any kind."   (Letter to Tayleur.)

On June 27, a week after the French royal family left Paris by night, Lindsey writes of the celebrations at the Crown and Anchor, which he proposed to attend :

" Although on Saturday there was a rumour that all was over with the Revolutionists, as the King, Queen, and royal family had escaped, but yesterday an account that they were re-taken and hopes that the Revolution would still maintain its ground, as I hope it will."   (Letter to Tayleur.)

At this time Lindsey was proposing to pay a second visit to his correspondent, W. Tayleur, at Shrewsbury, this time in company with Priestley.   The riots at Birmingham, July 14, 1791—the anniversary of the fall of the Bastille—led to the destruction of the two meeting-houses there, and of Priestley's house and library, on the 18th, three days after Lindsey had written to Tayleur of the visit to Shrewsbury.

The persecution of Dissenters by High Churchmen and the movements of Priestley are chronicled by Lindsey in some detail in the letter that follows.

On November 8, 1791, another celebration is recorded :

" You would see in the ' Morning Chronicle' how well everything went on at the London Tavern on the 4th Nov.   Much of it was due to our worthy chairman Mr. Walker of Manchester, who, with an ample, commanding figure, has a noble spirit to fill and animate it, and to the music being happily intermixed with the toasts, with some excellent songs, and the famous French Revolution tune, ' Ça ira,' seemed to inspire the whole company with a portion of their spirit.   It is very simple, with no variety, yet cheering in a high degree.   I thought I could observe several absent that used to be constant attendants, whom I suspected to keep away lest the court should suspect they had any connection with a thing called a revolution a hundred years ago.   The room, however, was very full, though not so crowded as the last two years."   (Letter to Tayleur.)

Writing, April 15, 1793, three months after the execution of Louis XVI. and two months after France had declared war on England, Lindsey remarks :

" Everything seems afloat in France, and I fear a sea of bloodshed and misery to be waded through before they can come to any good settlement.   I trust that in the result Divine Providence will secure to them their liberties, of which many among them have shown themselves unworthy."   (Letter to John Rowe.)

The influence of the war with France upon the position of Nonconformists in England is stated briefly by Lindsey :

" One is grieved that the war is likely to continue, as it will prevent the nation from cooling and returning to a better temper in laying the unavoidable evils and burdens that must result from it at the door of Dissenters of all sorts, instead of attending to the true cause of all our miseries." (Letter to W. Turner, jun., September 9, 1793.)

Beginning with an allusion to the fierce persecutions of the Unitarian and Independent Ministers, Fyshe Palmer and Winterbottom,[1] Lindsey, with a singular insight into the political situation, writes :

" If there was but a prospect of Mr. Fox's coming into power, who would certainly bring better principles with him, and require them to be acted upon ! But the day at present is far distant. I presume you know that there has lately been a sort of negociation of the Ministers with the Duke of Portland (as Mr. Pitt must be doubtless tired of the war, and wish others to take the load from his shoulders). Three Cabinet Ministers and patronage without end was offered, and without reserve, only Mr. Fox was to be excluded, for that the King could not bear him. It did not go on, however, as the Duke did not choose to submit to this last condition. But as he and other Whig Lords are much under Mr. Burke's direction, one can be surprised at nothing. They must have strange principles, or a strange itch after places not to stand aloof from a juncture with the present men in power." (Letter to Tayleur, December 2, 1793.)

The state of England as Lindsey sees it in 1794 was very gloomy.

" I am afraid nothing can be more black than the prospect of our affairs on the continent. England's sun, I fear, is certainly set for ever. And it may be, it will be better for the world, as we would not walk in its light nor suffer others." (Letter to Tayleur, December 8, 1794.)

[1] See pp. 94-7.

A month later he expresses his regrets that

" so presumptuous a young man as Mr. Pitt was ever placed at the helm in this country, which he has now, by his want of wisdom, brought to the very brink of ruin. The fascination, however, for him still seems to continue, and may go on until he has completed our fate. ' (Letter to John Rowe, January 22, 1795.)

On May 2, 1795, he writes of the progress of events to Tayleur :

" If we may believe the Ministerial prints and the conversation of those who would be thought to be in the secret of affairs, the National Convention has never been so near its fall as at present by the prodigious force which the Royalist party have in La Vendée, especially by the vast increase that has been given to it by us within these last two months, by the emigrants we have sent over with some troops of our own, and quantities of ammunition and stores. A priest of my acquaintance received a letter last week from a town in Poitou near the coast from an officer of family and fortune, who had landed out three weeks before from hence in company with other emigrants, telling him that he was very happily settled with his tenants all about, and that he would answer for it, that he might come over safely. I am, however, afraid that all our tampering, as hitherto, will only serve to keep up a most bloody war, which, without our interference, might never have begun, and certainly would have much sooner ended, as at present, we are the principals and prime agents in it. And the blessing of peace to the world is, by our means, withheld."

For some years after this, Lindsey's extant correspondence contains little reference to the war with France, save as it affected the persecution of Radicals in England. On July 7, in a letter to W. Turner, jun., he mentions a recent communication from Priestley and his " not having the least thought of visiting England till the storm of war has blown over, of which he had not much expectation."   Lindsey then adds :

"There is some ground of hope that we may be able to see Dr. P. sooner than he expected, if it be true what was yesterday said, that Buonaparte was returned to Paris with the preliminaries of a peace, and that Ulm was also in possession of the French.   For surely we shall not continue to carry on the war alone, if the Emperor close with the terms offered him."

Priestley did not again return to England, and when Lindsey died, November 8, 1808, in the eighty-sixth year of his age, the war with France was still raging.

To Lindsey, as to his young contemporaries the Lake Poets, the French Revolution had seemed big with all the hopes of man, and the disillusionment which followed was correspondingly severe, though it never drove him into the camp of the enemies of liberty.

The attitude of Lindsey and Priestley towards slavery has not always received the notice which it deserves.

Granville Sharpe's various actions at law had resulted in 1775 in the formulation of the principle " that as soon as any slave sets foot upon English territory he becomes free," and in 1787 the Society for the Abolition of Slavery was formed.

Writing to Tayleur, March 1, 1788, Lindsey says :

"When I was last in Johnson's shop, all the copies of his sermon on the Slave Trade which Priestley had sent up were sold, so that I hope it is well received as it greatly deserves. . . . I think his engaging in such a way against such a traffic will soften prejudices even with such very orthodox men as the worthy Granville Sharp, who hitherto has not allowed us salvation, unless we change our sentiments before we die, as he often expressed himself to Dr. Jebb."

The nature of the opposition which this great reform encountered is plain from Lindsey's letter to W. Turner, jun., May 4, 1792 :

" It will be some surprise perhaps to you though not to us to see that in the debate in the Lords House here yesterday, one of the Royal Dukes declared himself to be against the abolition of the trade of dealing in human flesh.   It is said, unless they should think better of it, that both the Prince of Wales, Duke of York and Gloucester will also give their votes against it.   To say nothing more of it, such conduct in them is certainly impolitic at this juncture."

The following day Lindsey wrote to Tayleur :

" You would be surprised at the Duke of Clarence joining Lord Stormont and the Chancellor in declaring himself against the abolition of the trade in human flesh. But they say even the other Royal Dukes will apppear against it.   The reason you will be at no loss to conjecture. . . . You see what an interdict the Minister put on all attempts to reform our body politic the other day.   He must know best what he has to do.   But this has been thought inconsistent in him, because it is acting so directly in the face of his own self in the setting out on his political career.   Some will have it that it was to conciliate matters with a great personage, who has taken amiss his going so far in reprobating the Slave Trade."

The last paragraph refers to Pitt's general support of Wilberforce and the party of emancipation, and, in particular, to his recent eloquent speech in support of the motion for the abolition of the slave trade.   The " attempts to reform the body politic " led to the prosecution of some of Lindsey's friends and correspondents.

Providence to spare him, as he is likely to be an instrument of great good in that country. . . ." (Letter to W. Turner, jun., March 24, 1794.)

Writing to John Rowe (January 23, 1795), Lindsey tells how the exiles fared on the journey.

" Mr. Joyce told me this morning that he had that day seen a letter from Margarot to a friend in London which mentioned, what I was sorry to hear, that there had actually been a mutiny on board the 'Surprize,' and that the ringleaders, whose names he does not tell, were in irons ; adding that Messrs. Palmer and Skirving were under some slight confinement for being privy to the intent, and that all of them were to undergo a trial when they arrived at Botany Bay."

The actual facts are related in a letter from Palmer to Lindsey, printed by Belsham, written from New South Wales, and dated September 15, 1795:

" The master [of the vessel] accused me and Mr. Skirving of hiring people to murder him and the principal officers.   He pitched on some unhappy people as our associates. . . . In the torrid zone, Mr. Skirving and I were shut up in a box six feet square, and not suffered to pass the threshold . . . The pretended associates . . . were flogged and illegally reduced to half allowance.   They were loaded with sixty pounds weight of irons, and all chained to an iron bar and exposed on the poop all weather in that dreadful temperature . . . When I landed six or seven people went voluntarily to a magistrate, and swore that C. (the master) offered them great rewards if they would swear that I and Mr. Skirving hired them to murder him and the principal officers, that he held a pistol in his hand and threatened to shoot some if they did not. . . ."

It was plainly not the intention of those who exiled Palmer that he should return.   Unhappily, on his return journey he fell into the hands of the Spanish, being driven by storms to land at the Ladrone Islands. Here dysentery again laid him low, and he died June 2, 1802.

The release of Winterbottom from prison after serving his sentence is announced in a letter to John Rowe (November 27, 1797), who is informed that " Mr. Winterbottom will soon be married to a modest but sickly young woman, whom I have sometimes seen in prison with him." A letter from Winterbottom (August 31, 1802) expressed his gratitude to Lindsey for all his kindness, and announced that his two eldest boys had been named after him and Mrs. Rayner, their father's benefactors.

CHAPTER V

LINDSEY AND HIS CONTEMPORARIES

NOT the least interesting feature of Lindsey's letters are the allusions to his contemporaries.

WILLIAM DODD

" You will have heard that the famous Dr. Dodd has been dismissed from being King's Chaplain for offering, by his wife, £3000 to the Lord Chancellor's lady to procure for him the living of St. George's, Hanover Square, which Dr. Moss is to vacate." (Letter to W. Turner, sen., February 9, 1774.)

Three years later, Dodd forged a bond for £4200 in the name of his former pupil, Lord Chesterfield, and was executed, despite numerous petitions in his behalf, one of which was written by Dr. Johnson.

DR. JOHNSON

Writing nineteen days after the death of the great lexicographer, Lindsey says :

" It would seem that the late Dr. Johnson by his parting advice to Sir Joshua Reynolds was grown Arian at last—as it was to read Dr. Clarke's works and not paint on Sundays." (Letter to Tayleur, January 1, 1785.)

The second injunction seems to have been given but not the first. Boswell says Johnson requested three things of Sir Joshua Reynolds: To forgive him £30, which he had borrowed of him; to read the Bible; and never to use his pencil on Sundays. Lindsey's reference to Clarke is apparently based on facts reported also by Boswell. Dr. Brocklesby says: "He pressed me to study Dr. Clarke and to read his sermons. I asked him why he pressed Dr. Clarke, an Arian. 'Because,' said he, 'he is fullest on the propitiatory sacrifice.'" Possibly Lindsey's informant was his friend Dr. Heberden, a member of Essex Street Chapel and a patron of Priestley, one of the most famous physicians of the eighteenth century, who attended Dr. Johnson, and to whom Johnson bequeathed a book " to keep as a token of remembrance."

JOHN WESLEY

Lindsey's opinion of Wesley and the Methodist movement is expressed in several letters. On December 11 he mentions:

" Mr. Coulthurst of Cambridge, a vehement Trinitarian, and one of those who are reckoned Methodists, of which there are not a few in the Colleges of Sidney, Clare Hall, Trinity Hall and Magdalen."

Writing to Tayleur, April 2, 1791, a month after John Wesley's death, he says:

" You will see in Mr. John Wesley's funeral sermon, if that be a true sample, that the doctrine of the founders is become much more liberal and rational than it was wont to be, though still retaining some of their peculiarities. But the concluding part, which contains an account of their old father, as they call him, for some days before he went out of the world, is far more unscriptural and enthusiastic, but it seems to have been put upon the pious old man by the zealous and devout women that were around him. Dr. Priestley may have told you that we expect a free and unprejudiced account of him from one that was formerly in connection with him as a preacher, but now is in the established church—a Mr. Hampson."

John Wesley's funeral sermon was preached by John Whitehead, M.D., and went through four editions. Lindsey uses the word "enthusiastic" in the sense it bore in the eighteenth century. Johnson defined "enthusiasm" as "a vain belief of private revelation; a vain confidence of divine favour or communication," and quotes Locke as saying, "Enthusiasm is founded neither on reason nor divine revelation, but rises from the conceits of a warmed or overweening brain."

Lindsey met John Hampson during a stay at Tunbridge Wells, and conversed with him freely on religious subjects. He describes him in a letter to Tayleur, September 20, 1790, as

"formerly in Mr. Wesley's connection, but, resisting some of his arbitrary decrees and being unacceptable, withdrew himself, and is now a free enquirer and nearly a perfect Unitarian in chains which he cannot well shake off."

The conversation took place shortly before Hampson was ordained in the Church of England. Hampson's *Life of Wesley* (June 1791), "mainly written and in great part printed before Wesley's death, was really the work of his father, who had left Methodism from disappointment at not being included in the legal hundred." The *Life* is not a favourite with the Wesleyans. On

January 5, 1792, Lindsey tells us something of what preceded the publication of the later and more official life of Wesley :

" There are great divisions among J. Wesley's followers. A large party under Dr. Coke have written to Dr. Whitehead to insist on their seeing the life of Mr. Wesley which Dr. W. is compiling by desire of the Trustees (one of them Dr. C. himself), with the liberty of making such alterations as they shall judge proper. This not being granted, they are about to compile a life of their leader themselves. I was yesterday informed by a judicious person who had been that morning with Dr. Whitehead and conversed with him on the subject, that his life of Mr. Wesley will be well conducted, not too flattering, abounding with many curious particulars from letters, MSS., etc., particularly two little excellent MS. vols. of Meditations by old Mrs. Wesley, the mother of them all."

The *Life of Wesley*, by Coke and Moore, chiefly written by the latter, was published in 1792 under the authority of the Conference, but without access to the Wesley papers. Whitehead's *Life* came out from 1793-96, and then Moore, having seen most of the papers, published a new *Life* in 1824–25. The Rev. Alexander Gordon says : " No higher tribute can be paid to the excellence of Whitehead's work than the constant use which Moore makes of it, frequently and without acknowledgement adopting its language."

JOHN JEBB

John Jebb (1736–86), Fellow of Peterhouse, first exhibited Unitarian opinions in his lectures on the New Testament in Cambridge in 1770. He took part in the Feathers Tavern Petition, and resigned his preferments in September 1775. Lindsey, as we have seen, failed to induce him to become his colleague. In politics he was a Radical, and in prison-philanthropy a pioneer. Jebb was one of Lindsey's correspondents, and a lifelong friend. Belsham made considerable use of Lindsey's letters to Jebb.

A letter to W. Turner, sen., January 5, 1774, a month after Lindsey's withdrawal from the Church, mentions Jebb's interest in his farewell address to his parishioners at Catterick :

" I must not omit to tell you that Mr. Jebb and some other Cambridge friends are so partial to the *Farewell Address* that, though it is entirely local in itself, they are persuaded it will be of use to be published, and therefore I have recommended it to Mr. Johnson, to whom I had given it."

Jebb was a friend of Tayleur before Lindsey, and Lindsey's first letter to the latter, August 5, 1775, intimates that Tayleur's name was always mentioned whenever he met Jebb. Of Jebb's interests after he left Cambridge we learn something from a letter to Tayleur, September 14, 1776 :

" That most worthy man and our common friend Mr. Jebb will give private lectures on the New Testament to enable him to support the expenses of living in Town, and pursuing Physic. His father has one thousand a year, no other child but a younger son well provided for, yet allows his eldest nothing, approving his principles but disapproving his conduct."

Lindsey occasionally joined Jebb in attending his medical lectures—once, at least, with disastrous results for both.

" I have been ill and confined. The worthy Mr. Jebb worse, and in imminent danger. We both got our colds, which brought on fevers, at the same time, in attending a lecture on Anatomy, when a stream of cold air blew upon us. He is now recovering."

Jebb graduated M.D. at St. Andrews on March 18, 1777, and was admitted licentiate by the London College of Physicians three months later.

" The excellent Dr. Jebb has just left me. He harasses himself too much with his studies, and attention to his new profession. But *quicquid vult, valde vult* is his noble character." (Letter to Tayleur, June 29, 1778.)

It was to Jebb that Lindsey owed his introduction to Tyrrwhitt.

" Yesterday just as I was sitting down to write to you, our friend Dr. Jebb came in with Mr. Tyrwhitt, the latter of whom I had never seen before, and we spent the remainder of the day together. Mr. T. is, as Dr. Jebb says, who well knows him, a person the most skilled in the Scriptures of anyone he knows, of various learning besides, and unspotted character. He showed his great integrity by refusing the offer of a great prelate some years ago, and lately by resigning his Fellowship of Jesus College in Cambridge, because he could not read or attend the prayers of the Church to which his place bound him. He is still residing in College, though he has quitted his Fellowship." (Letter to Tayleur, August 26, 1778.)

Jebb was a member of Essex Street Chapel.

" He never misses our Chapel twice a day, but on Sunday last, was engaged by his Uncle Sir Richard Jebb, who was ill, to visit some of his patients, which he could not decline." (Letter to Tayleur, December 3, 1778.)

Lindsey frequently lamented Jebb's immersion in politics, because of its withdrawing him from biblical and theological work.

" Dr. Jebb is still confined to his bed. . . . If he recovers, I wish he may abandon politics, in which he is sincere and aims at the public good, but hardly any else, I fear. Of all the persons I ever conversed with, he has the most critical knowledge of the Scriptures, and the best method of interpreting them." (Letter to Tayleur, December 10, 1782.)

" I cannot say that Dr. Jebb appears to me in so good a way at present, though he thinks he gains ground. But with regard to what you and I wish him wholly to lay aside all perplexity about, I am afraid—*non ipsa in morte reliquet*." (Letter to Tayleur, June 28, 1784.)

Jebb died of decline on March 2, 1786. His works were edited with a *Memoir* by Dr. Disney, Lindsey's colleague.

" I think Dr. Disney has acquitted himself very well in his *Memoirs of Dr. Jebb* and publication of his works. I am endeavouring that his criticisms and illustrations of Scripture may not be lost. . . . Mrs. Jebb very prudently gave up her groundless scruples, and is happy in the addition she will receive from the publication of the Dr.'s works to her income, not less than £800. Dr. Jebb behaved unworthily to the last, and left her only one hundred pounds, which was more a debt than a favour." (Letter to Tayleur, June 9, 1787.)

WILLIAM ROBERTSON, D.D.

William Robertson (1705–83), whom Lindsey calls "the father of Unitarian Nonconformity," was induced to resign his Irish preferment in 1764 by reading the *Free and Candid Disquisitions*, which advocated a scriptural subscription as sufficient for clergy of the established church. In 1768 he was appointed Master of the Wolverhampton Grammar School. Eight years later, Lindsey tells Tayleur :

" I have had the satisfaction of hearing from that most excellent person and confessor good Dr. Robertson of Wolverhampton, that it (the *Sequel to the Apology*) has brought him over *ad castra Socini*." (September 14, 1776.)

Lindsey's attempt to secure Robertson in 1778 as his colleague at Essex Street Chapel has already been noted. When in town Robertson occasionally stayed with Lindsey.

" Last week good Dr. Robertson of Wolverhampton was with us. He takes Town on his way home from Bath, and though with the infirmities of 76 and a constitution broken by the gout, he is still able to walk about, and be pleased with, and please, his friends, with his benign, placid countenance—the index of his mind and cheerful conversation." (Letter to Tayleur, September 29, 1781.)

A pleasing picture of Robertson is also presented, June 10, 1783, after his death on the previous May 20.

" His increasing infirmities had for a few years past made life very painful to him. But his liveliness and cheerfulness never forsook him. Just two days before he died, he wrote a letter to a lady, a friend of his in Town, which went through my hands, with a sprightfulness of fancy like one of twenty-five." (Letter to Tayleur.)

In his *Address to the Students of Oxford and Cambridge* (1788) Lindsey thus alludes to the book which led Robertson at an advanced age to leave the Church. " Somewhat less than forty years ago was published *Free and Candid Disquisitions relating to the Church of England*. In this design were embarked some persons of the laity of great learning and worth, and some highly estimable clerical characters, but we have never yet been made acquainted with their names." Mr. Colligan (*The*

Arian Movement in England, 1913) observes : " The authors of *Free and Candid Disquisitions* have not been identified, and it was not discovered until the beginning of the nineteenth century that Jones (of Alconbury) had edited it." Jones' editorship was disclosed in the *Monthly Repository* of 1807. Lindsey, as early as October 1, 1787—the year before he wrote the *Address to the Students* —was acquainted with the name of the editor of the book in question. In a letter of that date he mentions that

" John Jones, the very person who was one of the first movers, was entrusted with the secret and names of the contributors to the *Candid Disquisitions*, and was the editor of them. He was the *Night Thought* Dr. Young's curate, and died Vicar of Sheephall. He has left his MSS. to the Dissenters' Library in Red Cross Street, with an injunction not to be looked into of thirty years. These are believed to contain the history of the *Candid Disquisitions* and all secret ecclesiastical history of his own times."

Mr. Colligan remarks of the Jones MSS. : " Many of the notes are written upon the edges of newspapers and book advertisements, and imply that economy was a necessary virtue in the home of this poor but scholarly clergyman."

FRANCIS BLACKBURNE

Lindsey married in 1760 Hannah Elsworth, the step-daughter of Archdeacon Blackburne (1705–87), the author of *The Confessional*, published 1786, which had for its object the scheme suggested by the *Disquisitions* for a national church as a scriptural institution. The strained relations between Lindsey and his father-in-law which ensued upon Lindsey's conversion to Unitarianism are touched upon in his correspondence. On September 4, 1777, he writes to Tayleur :

" One happy circumstance has attended this excursion north, that a near relative of my wife's, an Unitarian himself, but who had very violently and inconsistently quarrelled and refused all communication with us on relinquishing Catterick, did at length yield to see us, and behaved with a good degree of kindness."

Writing six years later of the Archdeacon's refusal to join the Society for Promoting a Knowledge of the Scriptures (established 1783), promoted by Lindsey and his friends, though not confined to Unitarians, he speaks of his theological opinions :

" Archd. B. has returned rather a rough answer, but such is his nature, with those particularly whom he has some right to make free with. He has some sort of Trinity or Divinity of Christ ; what it is he would never reveal, which keeps him from all union with those he calls Socinians, whom he has sometimes declared that he hardly regards as Christians, and this keeps him aloof, though from our late more kind reception than usual, we thought it had been wearing off."

EDMUND LAW (BISHOP OF CARLISLE)

Amongst his many staunch friends in the established church Lindsey included Edmund Law (1703–87) and his son John, afterwards Bishop of Clonfert, of Killala, and of Elphin. Speaking of the seventh edition of Law's *Considerations on the State of the World with regard to the Theory of Religion*, originally published in 1745, Lindsey writes :

" The Bishop has done as he said, and changed his language with respect to Christ, but without giving any notice of it to his readers ; in which he has missed a fine opportunity of doing himself honour, and serving the cause of truth. I only looked to what he advances near the beginning of the ' Reflections on the Life and Character of Christ.' But in this there is a sad blunder. For the index stands unaltered, and still refers to Christ's original state, though the passage is quite different. . . . I had mentioned to our friend and relative at Richmond the change of sentiment in the Bp. of Carlisle, and that it would appear in the alteration made in his book. To which he replied yesterday : ' The old Bishop of Carlisle is no very respectable acquisition to any party, and if he ventures such a change in the dregs of life, it may merely be concluded that he has no longer any view to a transla- tion.' And yet he published his *Sleep of the Soul* before he was Bishop, for which, as I have often heard him say, Secker pursued him and opposed his promotion to the last." (Letter to Tayleur, June 5, 1784.)

The bishop died August 14, 1787, in the eighty-fifth year of his age. Writing to Tayleur (October 1, 1787), Lindsey says :

" The Bp. of Clonfert, the late Bp. of Carlisle's son, is in town, and has been here with us. I do not find from him that his father has left anything to be published. Indeed he did a great deal in his day for which he is much to be honoured. Archbishop Potter was his enemy for some free notions of exposition. Secker, still more, as the Bishop told me, for his *Sleep of the Soul* as being Socinian, and opposed his preferment on that account, and for not being orthodox concerning the divinity of Christ in his Reflections at the end of his *Theory of Religion*. And in the last edition of that work, he has purged it of many things, and stands forth of the Socinian sentiment. And in his College he certainly contributed to aid Jebb and others, and to countenance and promote liberality of sentiment through the University. If you ever look into the *Gentleman's Magazine,* you will be pleased to read his character in that of August —and especially the part that comes from Eugenius and signed J. J., that is John Jones, editor of *Candid Disquisitions.*"

EDWARD EVANSON

Of Edward Evanson (1731–1805), who resigned his living at Tewkesbury in 1778, Lindsey writes frequently. He entertained, however, little sympathy with his extreme biblical criticism. " I wish Mr. Evanson had omitted what he says of Matthew's Gospel, unless he had better supported it, and in what he appears most mistaken, as well as in so crudely cashiering parts of the last chapter of St. Mark." (Letter to Tayleur, December 18, 1777.)

Next year Lindsey paid a visit of which he writes to Tayleur :

" If I remember, in one of your former letters you asked me concerning Mr. Evanson, his temper, qualifications as a Teacher, etc. I was in the country lately for my health near Mitcham in Surrey, where he has taken a very healthy, commodious house. He has a sister, a very prudent person, not young, who keeps his house. He seems good-tempered, very conversible, and on very easy and affectionate terms with the only young boy that is his present pupil. It seems he formerly taught in an academy in this very place before he had a Church preferment, so that I suppose him extremely well qualified. . . . He intends to take no more than twelve pupils." (October 3, 1778.)

He gives another account of a visit to Evanson in December 1785, and on February 8, 1793, writes to Tayleur :

" You have probably heard of the most illiberal and unhandsome treatment which Mr. Evanson has experi-

that sort among the present generation, by the outcry that will be made against him . . . that he may see reason to lay aside other parts of the gospel, and, by degrees, both the Old and New Testaments." (Letter to Tayleur, December 30, 1783.)

The publication of the successive volumes of *The Theological Repository*, of which Tayleur was a patron, are noted by Lindsey, not without some expression of regret concerning Priestley's boldness of speech.

" He (Priestley) was much disappointed to find the *Repository* had sold so little—about a hundred of the first number, but none scarcely of the others. . . . I could wish we could have stopped the discussion of the miraculous conception, and some points that are to follow it. . . . There is cause to fear it will prejudice the sale of his valuable works." (Letter to Tayleur, April 3, 1785.)

In a letter to W. Turner, sen. (September 1, 1783), we catch a glimpse of another side of Priestley's activities.

" Mr. Burke, above a year ago, after having called upon Dr. Priestley, and seen his library, laboratory, and philosophic pursuits, with so much ease and cheerfulness carried on, reported him to all his friends as the most happy of men, and most to be envied. But Mr. Burke did not see, and would not perhaps have relished his Sunday work, which constitutes a chief part of his happiness. I was surprised on the Sunday afternoon, on going into the Vestry for my hat, to see near thirty young ladies, some of them, I was told, married, seated to be instructed in the principles of Christianity. This was the third class that had been before him that day, and this is his usual work every Sunday, added to his officiating to the whole congregation one part of it."

Priestley, after severing his connection with Lord Shelburne, had settled in Birmingham as minister of the New Meeting Chapel in 1780.

The following note refers to Mrs. Lindsey's interest in medicine, which she had practised with conspicuous success amongst her husband's parishioners at Catterick, and to Priestley's infirmity of speech. For many years, as Lindsey's letters show, his wife regularly prescribed for Priestley in matters of diet and the like, and to her, as we learn, Priestley " listened much in medicine."

" I must add that the Doctor's letter makes him far from well, so that my wife, in her friendly zeal and love for him, has written him a medical letter. . . . One fact I will give you in his own words ; but you will not mention that we correspond on such subjects. Having mentioned his reading aloud sometimes to Mrs. Priestley and a lady their guest, he adds, " I have found it useful to counteract my tendency to stammering, which has been very distressing to me of late, so that I have almost dreaded going into the pulpit. Yesterday I had great difficulty in getting through my work, though I have only one catechizing, and not three as in the summer." (Letter to Tayleur, November 29, 1788.)

His impediment of speech Priestley mentions several times in his autobiography, and states that he inherited it from his family. Lindsey interested himself in procuring patrons for his friend's publications, and, in a letter to Tayleur (April 24, 1784), laments the loss, by death and otherwise, of such patronage.

" I am very sorry that Dr. Priestley has found the contributions to his philosophical experiments fall off so much these two years past. Sir Geo. Saville had some- how or other been three years in arrears. I had men- tioned it to him, but he seems to have quite forgotten at last. His subscription was £10 per annum. . . . Others have been taken away. I have mentioned this thing to some who have useless thousands a year, but they have no heart, or are afraid, as churchmen and politicians, of encouraging heresy; ignorant of what would be their greatest honour now and ever, and one of the noblest uses of their wealth."

Priestley's relations with the political leaders of the day are touched upon in a letter to Tayleur (May 4, 1782).

" Dr. Priestley, reading one passage of the letter I received yesterday, wished me to say that he thought as well of the public character and enterprise of Mr. Fox as of those of his competitor ; that he had signed their address because all about him did, and, it being then his opinion that an aristocratic faction intended to tyrannize over king and people ; but he felt awkward in his present situation and believed it would not be long before he was in opposition again. Another person is persuaded that if Dr. P. had known facts, he would not have signed any such address nor have contributed to the national insanity in depressing characters, who were acting the parts of true friends to their country, and to Whig principles, and, on that very account and on that only, were the objects of One Man's unrelenting hatred, in whose good graces, with a full concurrence with them, is the E. India Bill. They had every reason to think themselves established till within eight hours of this discussion, till four o'clock of the day when the Seals were sent for at midnight. Mr. Pitt will have his hearty approbation, however, if he brings good to the country out of these confusions, but he fears a further scourge is intended for us."

Priestley, as the letter indicates, had signed one of the numerous addresses to the King applauding his action in dismissing the famous, or infamous, coalition of Fox and North, after the rejection by the Lords of Fox's India Bill. The defeat of the coalition marked the high-water mark of the monarch's personal rule, and from it dates the first Ministry of William Pitt, then a young man of twenty-four, which lasted more than seventeen years. The " One Man " in Lindsey's letter is the King, and " another person " is probably Lindsey himself.

Of the controversy between Priestley and Horsley, Lindsey writes (October 18, 1783) :

" Our friend Dr. Priestley has been drawn out to sea by the adverse power and violent storms and tempests conjured up against him, but he will ride out of them all triumphantly." (Letter to W. Turner, jun.).

Four and a half years later, he notes the effects of the controversy on the fortunes of Horsley.

" It is said with pretty good certainty that Dr. Horsley is to be the new Bishop, for which assuredly he may thank Dr. Priestley." (Letter to W. Turner, jun., February 4, 1788.)

" Bp. Hurd and the Chancellor, to gratify a great personage, as it is said, who is not very fond of Dissenters, and least of all of Dr. Priestley, are the promoters of Dr. Horsley to a bishopric ; a promotion, however, which I am told, is very displeasing to many upon the bench." (Letter to Tayleur, March 1, 1788.)

The growing antipathy towards Priestley on the part of his opponents is reflected in expressions of opinion, which Lindsey reports respecting his friend's sermon in connection with the anniversary of Hackney College, preached at Old Jewry, April 27, 1791.

" Two anecdotes concerning the sermon at the Old Jewry you will be pleased with. A great number of the ministers of the Independents as well as the Church of England were present. One of the former, when the whole was over, said to one that stood next him, ' Well, it must be said he fears neither God nor man.' Another, on the idolatry of Jesus Christ being named as one of the present great corruptions of Christianity, said to some about him, ' He ought to be sent to Newgate for that.'" (Letter to Tayleur, May 7, 1791.)

Fourteen days later, he writes again to Tayleur :

" Concerning the very valuable College sermon, you will not wonder it is spoken against, but would hardly expect that there should have been any thought of calling the preacher to account for it. Such thoughts, however, have been entertained, and only a week ago, two of the first rank in the law expressed themselves in that way towards Dr. P. to a friend of his not much inferior to themselves."

In the eventful month of July 1791, when Priestley was destined to suffer the loss of his library and apparatus at the hands of a Birmingham mob, and was driven to flee for his life, he and Lindsey, as we have seen, had arranged to visit their common friend at Shrewsbury. Writing to Tayleur (June 27, 1791), seventeen days before the riots broke out, Lindsey says :

" If I can accomplish it, my wife proposes, to prevent your being too much cumbered, that she will remain at Birmingham, and Dr. Priestley and I press forward to stay a day or two with you at Shrewsbury. We propose setting for the north, if nothing unforeseen happen, the last day in July."

The next letter records the reason for the failure of this plan.

" We are at length returned out of the North, not without many regrets that we could not make Shrewsbury on our way, as was originally intended, and formerly accomplished. . . . It was a great pleasure to find Dr.

Priestley well and cheerful as ever in the midst of all the vile calumnies daily contrived against him, added to the outrages of his enemies and their abettors throughout the kingdom. On Thursday last, when we came to Town, and first saw him, he had received letters from one of his friends at Birmingham, just to show himself for one day, and go to see his daughter. But the next day a letter came from his son William representing the state of the town in a more unfavourable view. . . . He does not now propose to pass through Birmingham, but to go another way to Mr. Finch's." (Letter to Tayleur, September 12, 1791.)

The plans and movements of Priestley are set forth in the letters that follow :

" Dr. Priestley was very well yesterday, and I expect him to-day, as also to preach for me to-morrow, which he did the Sunday before ; but the day was so exceedingly rainy we had a very thin audience. . . . He is very busy in fitting up his laboratory and the house he has taken at Lower Clapton. . . . This day week he sent an answer to a very affecting address from his people with a very many signatures, pressing his return among them, and promising him security and liberty, the latter, I fear, more than they could answer for. With much reluctance he sent a negative. . . . Many at Hackney are endeavouring to procure his being elected in Dr. Price's room, and a majority are for him, but two-thirds, by a former agreement, are to decide. . . . If this should not take place, it is proposed by several friends to erect an Unitarian Chapel, wherein he will officiate with a liturgy, to which a great majority are disposed." (Letter to Tayleur, October 15, 1791.)

Four days later we read :

" Dr. P. has just come in. . . . He has a letter to-day from Mr. Russell, signifying to him, that himself and the nothing, particularly of the above named authors, is to be seen. And the clergy of the Cathedral have taken to preaching up the doctrine of the Trinity, and Athanasius' creed is resumed again in places where it had been omitted for many years past. Dr. Priestley was made uneasy yesterday by the account of his second son's naturalization in France, which he read for the first time in the *Morning Chronicle* of yesterday. . . . He went to France to be in a mercantile house, but I should not be surprised to hear that he followed the camp. The whole of the circumstance will furnish Mr. Burke and the public prints with ample materials against the Doctor and all Dissenters, particularly Unitarians."

Benjamin Carpenter (1752–1816) was minister of Stourbridge Presbyterian Chapel, 1778–95, and again 1807–16.

Timothy Kenrick (1759–1804) was minister at George's Meeting, Exeter, from 1785, and conducted an academy in the city from 1759 until his death, having previously declined an invitation to the Divinity chair in the Manchester Academy.

The same theme (the hostility manifested towards Dissenters) is pursued in a letter to Tayleur (February 8, 1793), wherein Lindsey foresees the possible migration of Priestley to America, an event which took place little more than a year later.

" I am sorry to hear that a portion of the same spirit had shown itself at Shrewsbury, which had broken out at other places, and that Mr. Rowe was in some danger from the threats of the populace. I will, however, hope that his own most worthy character and your venerable name and high estimation will be his protection till the storm is over. It is a great satisfaction that everything is quiet in this respect throughout this monstrous city and its environs ; and although Dissenters are aspersed and detested as much as in the latter end of Queen Anne's reign, no outward violence is offered or seems meditated against them or their places of worship. . . . I presume you are acquainted with the design of a migration to America, entertained by several Dissenting families in Lancashire, whose situation has been rendered very uneasy to them of late and is not likely to mend. . . . Mr. Toulmin of Taunton expressed great anxieties on the prospect of parting with his son. I shall be glad, if it may be some consolation what I told him, that Dr. Priestley has reconciled himself to his eldest son's crossing the Atlantic, and that who knows but that he and the Doctor years hence may find, if not an asylum, yet very peculiar satisfaction and joy in visiting their sons, and beholding their increase and happiness and great usefulness."

Joshua Toulmin (1740–1815), Dissenting historian and biographer, was minister of Colyton, 1761, Taunton, 1765, and from 1804 until his death, of the New Meeting, Birmingham. He was an intimate friend and correspondent of Lindsey, and on the representation of Priestley, Price, and Lindsey received the degree of D.D. from Harvard College in 1795. At his death, in accordance with his wish, his pall was supported by six ministers of different denominations. His son Harry was minister of Monton (1786), Chowbent (1788). He emigrated to the United States, 1793, and became Secretary to the State of Kentucky, Judge of the Mississippi Territory, and member of the General Assembly of the State of Alabama.

The impending departure of Priestley for America is mentioned in a letter to W. Turner, jun., March 24, 1794 :

" You will be glad to hear that Dr. Priestley keeps up his spirits and enjoys entire health in the midst of his great

" We are all anxious to hear the result of the threatened invasion. I have some faint hopes it will not be undertaken, at least upon England. What confusion and distress would it not occasion, in the most favourable issue ? How enviable is our situation compared to yours ? God preserve you, my friend, from the general calamity. Our only consolation must arise from regarding the hand of God in all events, confident that the issue will be right and good."

RICHARD PRICE

With Dr. Price, Lindsey had much in common in politics and in theology, despite their differences in Christology, and the two men were firm friends. Price's doctrinal opinions are mentioned in what follows, together with his belief in frankness of speech on the part of Unitarians.

" Good Dr. Price, though an Arian, is one of the strictest Unitarians I know. On this account, he holds the worship of the Church of England to be wholly idolatrous, and scruples not to speak of it as such. What makes me thus abruptly mention him is my having been with him a few days ago, when he was very low-spirited on account of the poor state in which the Rational Dissenters were, both in the country as well as in the Town. Their congregations are crumbling away to nothing— the lower part joining the Methodists, those more at ease, the Church ; all which, he said, would not have happened if Unitarians had informed their people properly, and spoken of the established worship as became them." (Letter to Tayleur, June 28, 1782.)

An interesting detail relating to one of Price's works is related in a letter to Tayleur, September 22, 1784.

" Dr. Price has nearly printed off his *Advice to the American States*. He gives in it a letter of Mons. Turgot to himself on the subject—a very great man among them, Controller General, deceased a few years since. M. Turgot's friends made a difficulty in permitting it to be printed, but have at last assented only on leaving out a few things. One omission insisted on is very curious. I think it is the Maryland State which alone insists on the chief magistrate subscribing their belief of the divinity of Jesus. This Mons. Turgot spoke of as most narrow and bigoted and not to be endured, but his family in France have insisted on this part being left out."

Turgot (1727–81) was the famous statesman and financier, friend of Voltaire and Condorcet, who might have saved the French monarchy and averted the revolution if he had been permitted to carry through his reforms, and not dismissed by the King in deference to his enemies in 1776.

A difference of opinion between Lindsey and Price, with evidence of Priestley's influence over the former, may be seen in a letter to Tayleur, June 26, 1788.

" A letter or two passed between good Dr. Price and me on occasion of the *Vindiciæ (Address to the Students of Oxford and Cambridge)*. He found fault that I had given cause to think that in all points he agreed with Bp. Butler, and that I should have mentioned his differing from him on the point of worshipping Christ, and in respect of the divine character and government, and that I showed a want of candour in charging Arians with resisting an evidence that was insurmountable. But I have entirely satified him, I believe, in this last point that I had no such intention, and have told him that if ever the tract comes to a second edit'on, I will omit his name where I spoke of Bp. Butler, and am persuaded that we are now the best of friends. . . . There is no book which has been more read, or done more good to the Unitarian cause than Dr. Price's Sermons in this part of the world. But I confess myself daily inclining towards Socinianism. I cannot resist the force of Dr. Priestley's reasoning. There are, however, some difficulties which still perplex me. Many of my friends are in the same situation with myself, *i.e.* they are gradually losing their Arian ideas."

In a letter to Tayleur (April 27, 1791), after speaking of the funeral of Price, Lindsey pays tribute to his character and influence :

" Yesterday we attended the funeral of the excellent Dr. Price. Dr. Kippis spoke over the grave, which I could not well hear, but the scene itself was most instructive. . . . I reckon it a great privilege that he died in the midst of his usefulness, before great infirmities came on. His private and public virtues considered, I do not think that Dissenters had ever his equal."

WILLIAM FREND (1757–1841)

Of William Frend, Lindsey makes frequent mention. Frend suffered for his conversion to Unitarianism in 1787 by his removal from the office of Tutor at Jesus College, Cambridge, in the following year, and for his political opinions, expressed in his *Peace and Union Recommended*, 1793, by his expulsion from the University. He married in 1808 a daughter of the Rev. Francis Blackburne, granddaughter of Archdeacon Blackburne, Lindsey's father-in-law. His eldest daughter married Professor Augustus De Morgan. Their first son was William Frend De Morgan, the novelist, and their third son, Edward Lindsey, derived his second name from Theophilus Lindsey, his mother's great-uncle.

Writing to Tayleur (December 31, 1787), Lindsey names Frend for the first time.

" Mr. Frend, a Kentish gentleman, who is a Fellow of

Jesus, was at our chapel yesterday, and I had some conversation with him afterwards. I think I told you that he had not long ago given up the living of Maddington (Sir John Hyde Cotton's seat), near Cambridge : not very great in value, but much sought after, as so securely to be served from College. How far his scruples go, I cannot tell, but by his great ardour of mind, and being a Tutor of the College, he may be of great service. He does not seem to be more than 27 or 28 years old. One proof of his, and his friends' zeal at Cambridge —no heretical books are admitted on the shelves of the two principal booksellers. They have therefore engaged an inferior one to have a shelf for them, and have undertaken to support him."

The progress of Frend's views in the Unitarian direction and what followed are in due course set down by Lindsey.

" The Master of the College, Dr. Beadon, acquainted him (Frend) about a week ago, that after the public declaration that he had made of his religious sentiments in such a way, he would not allow him to remain a Tutor in the College, but, as it would require time to settle accounts with his pupils, he should consent to his continuing, if he pleased, to Michaelmas next. Dr. Beadon came to Town immediately after this. It is believed at Cambridge that he consulted with, and was directed by, the Archbp. and Bishops in London how to act upon the occasion, and, with that view, Mr. Frend will be permitted to enjoy his Fellowship without molestation." (Letter to Tayleur, May 2, 1788.)

Six months later, Lindsey writes :

" You would see in the papers Mr. Frend of Jesus College, Cambridge's statement of his own case, which I handed to the press for him. I am glad he does not tamely give up his Tutorship, as standing out a little will make the cause for which he is removed from it more attended to. A few weeks ago, Mr. Lambert of Trinity College wrote to me, ' Our friends here, Tyrwitt and Frend, are in good spirits. The lions begin to roar from their pulpits. The Divinity of Jesus was maintained on Sunday in full force by Mr. Boycott of Caius College, and yesterday Dr. Kipling, one of the Divinity Professors, thought proper to give the heretics a drubbing. But I am sorry to tell you that I am of opinion that if they thought proper to proceed to a more public censure of Mr. Frend instead of making him give up the tuition, there is a majority in the University who would gladly join in inflicting it." (Letter to Tayleur, June 26, 1788.)

The writer whose words are quoted was James Lambert, Greek Professor at Cambridge, 1771–80, who adopted Unitarian opinions and never accepted preferment in the Church, though retaining his Fellowship until his death in 1823.

Lindsey next describes the persecution of Frend for his religious opinions.

" The Master of his College (Jesus), Dr. Beadon, has fixed up a paper in the Hall and in the Chapel, appointing two new Tutors. But I have not heard that any other steps have been taken, and Mr. Frend is waiting the event. It is thought the little publication I have sent you will tend to exasperate matters, and many expect they will try to eject him from his Fellowship, while others suppose they will let him alone for fear of the noise it will make, as he will not certainly be silent under persecution. Mr. Tyrwhitt, who still lives in the College, attending Commons, etc., will be no small check upon them, as his sentiments are so well known, and his character and connections very respectable, and his fortune also, since his brother's death, very ample. Mr. Frend was of Christ College, but removed to Jesus for a Fellowship, and some of the current wit about him is—Friend of Christ, Friend of Jesus, Friend of the Devil." (Letter to Tayleur, October 7, 1788.)

The progress of the Cambridge controversy is reported by Lindsey to his correspondent :

" Enclosed are three copies of Mr. Frend's reply to Mr. Coulthurst. The controversy cannot but have the best effects on the University, and it was with great pleasure, about three weeks ago, that I heard Dr. Heberden remark, who has a son there, that Unitarianism was spreading among the young students. Mr. Coulthurst is a very good mathematician, but, like Prof. Waring, of the same University, who is reckoned the first mathematician of the age, he is a vehement Trinitarian. . . . He has preached another sermon at which Mr. Frend was present, and he is setting about an answer, but, as I think I told you, Sir, before, he sends it up to be printed here, as he is denied the University press." (Letter to Tayleur, December 11, 1788.)

Lindsey's tribute to Frend's fluency as an extemporaneous preacher has been already given (see p. 38). In letters to Rowe (May 7, 1793) and Tayleur (July 18, 1793) he describes the attacks made upon Frend for his political opinions :

" You will be glad to be informed that the shameful renewal of the attack upon Mr. Frend by the University, after his being tried and sentenced to rustication in his own College, is likely to come to nothing. On Friday last Mr. Frend was convened before the Vice-Chancellor's court and behaved with great courage and coolness and good sense. But the business was put off till Friday next by his objecting to the jurisdiction of the court in his case.

" On Saturday we set out for my friend's Mr. Reynold of Paxton. Perhaps, as it is not far from Cambridge, we

K

may see Mr. Frend. He has had a call for a second edition of his tract, for which he has been persecuted, *Peace and Union*, and has printed 1500. His own account of the Proceedings against him is in the press, and will make a good sized volume. I observe his adversaries have been before him in publishing their account of the business."

A few days later he writes again to his Shrewsbury friend :

" At my old College chum's, Mr. Reynolds of Paxton in Huntingdonshire, Mr. Frend from Cambridge met us, and passed much of the time with us. To all his other valuable parts and virtues, there is added an open, cheerful disposition, which renders his company very agreeable. He has not yet decided what steps to take. He is at present busy publishing his account of the Proceedings against him. . . . The Court of Delegates, to whom he appealed, confirmed the Vice-Chancellor's sentence. Some doubt of the Courts in Westminster Hall interfering on an appeal to them, as they may allege the affair to be an act of discipline, in the exercise of which the University is not to be interrupted."

Despite an unsuccessful appeal to the King's Bench which followed, Frend remained in possession of his Fellowship until he married, owing to a technicality which made the expulsion illegal.

Tom Paine (1737–1809)

The attitude of Lindsey towards Paine, the celebrated author of *The Rights of Man*, is rather carefully defined in his letters. Priestley and Price were friends and supporters of Paine, whose political opinions won also the approbation of Lindsey. Part I. of *The Rights of Man* was printed by Johnson, says Moncure Conway, "in time for the opening of Parliament (February), and only a few copies bearing his name found their way into private hands." Johnson took alarm at its contents and abandoned it. "J. S. Jordan consented to publish it, and Paine, entrusting it to a committee of friends, took his departure for Paris. From that city, he sent a brief Preface, which appeared with Jordan's first edition," March 13, 1791.

Lindsey must have been possessed of one of "the few copies" published by Johnson, for he writes to Tayleur, February 23, 1791 :

"Mr. Paine's book against Mr. Burke has some fine things upon the subject of universal toleration in religion, which must effect every mind, but the book is so entirely republican, though full of much excellent matter, and contains such reflections on the Brunswick princes, that Mr. Johnson, for whom it is printed, is advised not to sell it."

Lindsey's correspondent was, at least, as warm an admirer of the book as himself.

"I am as much an idolater of Mr. Paine's book as you are, and trust our nation will profit by it, but it would have been more read if some things towards the latter end had been omitted." (Letter to Tayleur, April 9, 1791.)

Lindsey was wrong as to the number of readers to whom the book would appeal, as indeed his next reference to it shows. Paine's Second Part was to appear about February 1, 1792. But the printer (Chapman) threw up the publication, alleging its "dangerous tendencies." It was consequently delayed until February 17, when it was published by Jordan. Again, Lindsey was one of the earliest readers of Paine, and acquainted with Part II. before it was offered to the general public. Writing to Tayleur, February 15, 1792, he speaks of the work as a whole, and of its probable influence for good :

" A gentleman, a few days ago arrived from the neighbourhood of Sheffield, says that there is a society of two thousand in that town, well-behaved men, most of them of the lower sort of workmen, who have regular meetings to discuss various subjects, particularly that of government. They had all of them read and approved Mr. Paine's *Rights of Man* half a year ago, which we heard of when in the North—but they are now printing a cheap copy to dispose. Mr. Paine's second volume, which I have just had a sight of, will fall in with and promote their speculations, and, indeed, must promote no small change in the minds of men, and, in time, on all the governments on the earth, when such plain, striking truths will probably be dispersed and adopted. Such just ideas of government make me look forward with satisfaction to this earth of ours, when they will probably be realized everywhere and wars be no more."

On September 13, 1792, Paine fled to France to escape arrest. He had just finished the first part of *The Age of Reason* when he was flung into prison upon the fall of his friends the Girondins (December 27, 1793). He remained in gaol ten months, and occupied himself with the composition of the second part of *The Age of Reason*. The first part was published on January 27, 1794. Lindsey comments upon it and upon Gilbert Wakefield's intemperate reply to it :

" Mr. Rowe will have told you of Mr. Thomas Paine's book called *The Age of Reason* pointed against all divine revelation. He seems to speak the sentiments of Robespierre and the present leaders in France. And it is a noble foundation which they have laid in the divine unity, and on a perfect liberty in religious matters. On this basis the gospel in time will be preached in its native simplicity, and firmly established in such a way as it never yet has been. To which Thomas Paine leads the way without intending it by exciting free enquiry. I wish Mr. Wakefield had taken more time in his answer to him, and been less abusive in some places, though he is candid in others." (Letter to Tayleur, May 29, 179–.)

Of *The Age of Reason*, Part II., published in 1795, Lindsey writes to John Rowe :

" Mr. Paine's second part of his *Age of Reason* is come. I have not read it, but expect, that like the former part, it will make many reject revelation, who took up the belief of it from others without enquiring into the grounds of its evidence for themselves." (October 26, 1795.)

Priestley's reply to *The Age of Reason* in 1794 was reprinted in London, 1796, with a Preface by Lindsey.

" It becomes me, now the main hindrance is removed, to acquaint you that for these last three weeks all the spare moments I could get have been spent in reprinting, by Mr. Johnson's means, Dr. Priestley's answer to Mr. Paine's *Age of Reason*, and in preparing a Preface for it in vindication of our friend's name, which I shall be happy if you approve." (Letter to Tayleur, May 2, 1796.)

In his Preface, Lindsey expresses his belief that Priestley, " frankly acknowledging those gross errors among Christians which Mr. Paine justly reprobates," " detects and plainly shows him his mistakes in everything of consequence which he has advanced against real Christianity. At the same time he pays tribute to Paine's " talent, perhaps above all other writers, of arresting the attention of his readers, and making them pleased and desirous of

Tutor. There were some objections at first on account
of his temper, as being haughty and contemptuous, and
ill to live with, chiefly drawn from the cast of his writings.
But I believe that accounts of him from different persons
that know him have removed the difficulty. . . . His
answer of Bp. Horsley just published is a very tart
one. At the end of it are his proposals for a translation
of the New Testament, which I hope meet with encouragement, as it cannot be doubted but it will be a
very great improvement of our present translation, from
his known abilities, and from his long having had the
matter in hand. I remember that when once I asked
the late Bp. Law to indulge me with a sight of the
alteration he had made in the English New Testament,
he told me that he had lent it to Mr. Wakefield."

One of the objections to Wakefield's appointment was
based on his neglect of public worship. At Warrington
he had occasionally attended the Church of England
services, " from an unconquerable aversion to the mode
of praying among Dissenters," as he confessed in his
Memoirs (published 1792), but later he abandoned the
practice almost wholly. In a subsequent letter describing
the opening of the session at Hackney, Lindsey observes
(September 20, 1790) :

" Mr. Wakefield was with his fellow-tutors, and, I
apprehend, convinced them that his manners are social
and agreeable, and that he is severe and formidable only
with his pen in his own hand."

Lindsey's hopes were not fulfilled. His next allusion
to the College mentions Wakefield's successor, John Pope,
and his colleague, Dr. Price, both of whom Wakefield
belaboured mercilessly in his *Memoirs*. The publication
by Wakefield of his tract on *Worship*, and the controversy
that followed, are also noted.

In January 1799 Wyvill defended, in a short pamphlet, the secession from Parliament of Fox and some of his chief supporters in both Houses.   Lindsey thus refers to the publication :

" Dr. Fenwick's judgment concerning the obnoxiousness of Mr. Wyvill's pamphlet has been confirmed by no reputable bookseller's venturing to undertake the publication.   Johnson's fate deters them all, added to the suspension of the Habeas Corpus Act, which I do not expect to see removed whilst I remain in the land of the living." (Letter to W. Turner, jun., January 1, 1799.)

Upon Lindsey's publication of his last work, *Conversations on the Divine Government*, Wyvill sent him an appreciative letter, May 31, 1802, which Belsham published in his *Memoir of Lindsey*.

A little earlier than this (December 1801) Lindsey suffered a severe attack of paralysis, from which, however, he made a good recovery.   On July 3, 1802, Priestley rejoiced to receive a letter from him, " written wholly with his own hand."   On February 3, 1804, Priestley himself died.   Lindsey lingered four years longer.   During the summer of 1808 his health rapidly declined.   He died November 3, 1808, in the eighty-sixth year of his age.

INDEX

THE END

Printed by R. & R. CLARK, LIMITED, Edinburgh.